Esteban Montejo: "This is not sad because it is true."

THE

AUTOBIOGRAPHY OF

A RUNAWAY

SLAVE

Esteban Montejo

EDITED BY *Miguel Barnet*

TRANSLATED FROM THE SPANISH

BY *Jocasta Innes*

MERIDIAN BOOKS

The World Publishing Company

NEW YORK AND CLEVELAND

A MERIDIAN BOOK

Published by The World Publishing Company
2231 West 110th Street, Cleveland, Ohio 44102
Published simultaneously in Canada by
Nelson, Foster & Scott Ltd.

First Meridian Printing—1969

Reprinted by arrangement with Pantheon Books,
a division of Random House, Inc.

Copyright © 1968 by The Bodley Head Ltd. Originally
published in Spanish as *Biografía de un Cimarron.*

Manufactured at World Publishing Press, a division of
The World Publishing Company, Cleveland, Ohio

Library of Congress Catalog Card Number: 68–25640

PRINTED IN THE UNITED STATES OF AMERICA

WORLD PUBLISHING
TIMES MIRROR

CONTENTS

Introduction

I FIRST met Esteban Montejo in the summer of 1963. He struck me as a lonely, aloof, almost severe character. He received me coldly and with considerable reserve. I wanted to meet this man of a hundred and five years because he had lived through experiences which seem extraordinary to people today. The most attractive of these, perhaps, was his time as a runaway slave in the forests of central Cuba.

With time and the requisite patience, I managed to get him to talk naturally and frankly, and these conversations became the material for a book about his life. I filled shoe-boxes with notes and filing cards, and taped a lot of our talks—somewhat haphazardly, I must admit. This took about two years. I wanted his story to sound spontaneous and as if it came from the heart, and so I inserted words and expressions characteristic of Esteban wherever they seemed appropriate. My particular concerns were the social problems of life under slavery, the promiscuity in the barracoons, Esteban's celibate life as a runaway and his part in the War of Independence, which he describes from a lively, personal angle—the anti-romantic, anti-ideological standpoint of a man who joined the fight purely from a hunger for freedom, without petty motives or the hope of easy privileges.

Esteban soon became the real author of this book. He was constantly looking at my notebook, and he almost forced me to write down everything he said. His vision of the creation of the universe particularly appealed to me because of its poetic, surrealist slant.

The need to check facts and dates which cropped up in these sessions of ours led me to conversations with other old men more or less his contemporaries. I pored over reference books and city records, and revised the whole period under review so that my questions should be as precise as possible. Not that this book is primarily a work of history—history merely enters it as the medium in which the man's life is lived.

I have necessarily had to paraphrase a good deal of what he told me. If I had transcribed his story word for word it would have been confusing and repetitive. I have kept the story within fixed time-limits, not being concerned to recreate the period in minute detail of time and place. I have concentrated on things like agricultural methods, ceremonies, fiestas, food and drink, although in many cases my informant was unable to remember precisely when he had been involved with them. I have checked the facts where they seemed important—as in the account of slavery and of the two wars, the Ten Years' War of Carlos Manuel de Cespedes and the War of Independence. Esteban's life in the forest is a remote and confused period in his memory.

This book helps to fill certain gaps in Cuba's history.

None of the orthodox, schematically-minded historians would ever have bothered with the experiences of a man like Esteban. But Esteban appeared on the scene as if to show that one voice from the heart of action is worth a vociferous chorus from the sidelines.

The war against Spain, our 'motherland', lasted almost a century. After the Haitian Revolution and the Negroes' seizure of power there, led by Toussaint L'Ouverture, the Spanish Government was forced to adopt measures to prevent a similar conflagration in Cuba. Nationalist feeling grew, and there were several important rebellions. Esteban refers to two of these. The first, which sprung from the *Grito de Yara** in 1868, was headed by a patriot from Bayamo, in Oriente Province, Carlos Manuel de Cespedes. This war, in which much of the Negro population was involved, was a strange, remote and disconcerting experience for Esteban, During that time, the decade from '68 to '78, he was a runaway in hiding in the mountains and he only occasionally heard a shot or caught sight of a platoon travelling across the plains. It was bewildering to see horses charging and men cutting each other's heads off with machetes and not knowing what it was all about. Esteban told me once that the experience was like standing drunk in front of the sea.

Then, in 1880, two years after the end of what Cubans call the Ten Years' War, the abolition of slavery was declared. Esteban left the forest and his celibate existence there, to take up a new life. The Ten Years' War was a

* Literally 'the Shout of Yara'. This refers to the patriotic outcry raised in the village of Yara which sparked off the Ten Years' War of Carlos Manuel de Cespedes.

failure for the Cubans, but at least slavery had been abolished.

Political turmoil continued. Cuba swarmed with different parties and factions. Men like Esteban wanted nothing less than total freedom: Cuba's independence of Spain and solid economic advantages. Consequently, whenever he mentions annexationism, the movement in favour of Cuba's annexation to the United States, or autonomism, which proposed that Spain should concede certain trading advantages on the island but keep political control, he does so in vague, pejorative terms. Independence, though, the one dignified solution, was the cause which united the whole revolutionary population of Cuba, including this one unknown man. On February 24th, 1895, the *Grito de Baire* was heard in a poor village in Oriente Province and gave birth to the War of Independence which freed Cuba from Spanish rule. Esteban talks, in his very subjective and individual way, of such great and distinguished figures as Máximo Gómez and Antonio Maceo, both generals in this war. Maceo was a Negro, and consequently Esteban's attitude to the two men differs widely, a fact which throws light on certain aspects of the war as well as on the racial attitudes he shared with other Negroes. He admired Maceo as much as he distrusted Gómez, whom he believed to be a puppet of the Americans.

During the war Esteban went through testing experiences. He first fought under bandit leaders who turned out traitors to the revolution, then under a more honest officer, but always in difficult and distracting circumstances. When the war ended the ex-slave, ex-runaway and ex-revolutionary was humiliated to see an unexpected and unpleasant development. The Americans intervened after the Cubans had fought and won the war and seized power for themselves. As a pretext for intervention they used the blowing up of their warship, the *Maine*, then at anchor in our waters. We believe that they blew up the ship themselves, and then accused Spain of having done so.

Esteban was further disillusioned to find himself the object of racial discrimination, and jobless, after having fought bravely and honourably. So he went back to the countryside, to his old life of cutting cane, clearing the ground and hunting pigs. But this did not break his spirit. He carried on the hard struggle for existence and overcame poverty and pain. Now, after forty years of retirement, he tells his life story, sitting in a leather chair, and stoutly maintains that he does not want to die so that he can take part in any battles to come. 'And I'm not going into the trenches,' he explains, 'or using any of those modern weapons. A machete will do for me.'

MIGUEL BARNET

PART I

SLAVERY

Life in the Barracoons

THERE are some things about life I don't understand. Everything about Nature is obscure to me, and about the gods more so still. The gods are capricious and wilful, and they are the cause of many strange things which happen here and which I have seen for myself. I can remember as a slave I spent half my time gazing up at the sky because it looked so painted. Once it suddenly turned the colour of a hot coal, and there was a terrible drought. Another time there was an eclipse of the sun which started at four in the afternoon and could be seen all over the island. The moon looked as if it was fighting with the sun. I noticed that everything seemed to be going backwards—it got darker and darker, and then lighter and lighter. Hens flew up to roost. People were too frightened to speak. Some died of heart failure and others were struck dumb.

I saw the same thing happen again in different places, but I never dreamed of trying to find out why. You see, I know it all depends on Nature, everything comes from Nature, even what can't be seen. We men cannot do such things because we are the subjects of a God; of Jesus Christ, who is the one most talked about. Jesus Christ wasn't born in Africa, he came from Nature herself, as the Virgin Mary was a señorita.

The strongest gods are African. I tell you it's certain they could fly and they did what they liked with their witchcraft. I don't know how they permitted slavery. The truth is, I start thinking, and I can't make head or tail of it. To my mind it all started with the scarlet handkerchiefs, the day they crossed the wall. There was an old wall in Africa, right round the coast, made of palm-bark and magic insects which stung like the devil. For years they frightened away all the whites who tried to set foot in Africa. It was the scarlet which did for the Africans; both the kings and the rest surrendered without a struggle. When the kings saw that the whites—I think the Portuguese were the first—were taking out these scarlet handkerchiefs as if they were waving, they told the blacks, 'Go on then, go and get a scarlet handkerchief', and the blacks were so excited by the scarlet they ran down to the ships like sheep and there they were captured. The Negro has always liked scarlet. It was the fault of this colour that they put them in chains and sent them to Cuba. After that they couldn't go back to their own country. That is the reason for slavery in Cuba. When the English found out about this business, they wouldn't let them bring any more Negroes over, and slavery ended and the other part began: the free part. It was some time in the 1880s.

I haven't forgotten any of this. I lived through it all. I even remember my godparents telling me the date of my birth. It was the 26th of December 1860, St Stephen's

Day, the one on the calendars. That is why I am called
Stephen. One of my surnames is Montejo, after my
mother who was a slave of French origin. The other is
Mera. But hardly anyone knows this. Well, why should
I tell people, since it is false anyway? It should really be
Mesa, but what happened is that they changed it in the
archives and I left it that way because I wanted two
names like everyone else, so they wouldn't call me
'jungle boy'. I stuck to this one and, well, there you are!
Mesa was the name of a certain Pancho Mesa who lived
in Rodrigo. It seems this gentleman cared for me after
I was born. He was my mother's master. I never saw him,
of course, but I believe this story because my godparents
told it to me, and I remember every word they told me.

My godfather was called Gin Congo and my god-
mother Susanna. I got to know them in the Nineties
before war began. An old Negro from their sugar
plantation who knew me gave me the introduction to
them, and took me to see them himself. I got into the
way of visiting them in Chinchila, the district where
they lived near Sagua la Grande. As I had never known
my parents, the first thing I did was ask about them, and
that was when I found out their names and other details.
They even told me the name of the plantation where I
was born. My father was called Nazario and he was a
Lucumi* from Oyó. My mother was Emilia Montejo.
They told me too that they had both died at Sagua. I
would very much like to have known them, but if I had

* Cuban name for a Negro slave who came from Nigeria or the Gulf
of Guinea.

[17]

left the forest to find them I would have been seized at once.

Because of being a runaway I never knew my parents. I never even saw them. But this is not sad, because it is true.

Like all children born into slavery, *criollitos** as they called them, I was born in an infirmary where they took the pregnant Negresses to give birth. I think it was the Santa Teresa plantation, but I am not sure. I do remember my godparents talking a lot about this plantation and its owners, people called La Ronda. My godparents were called by this name for a long time, till slavery left Cuba.

Negroes were sold like pigs, and they sold me at once, which is why I remember nothing about the place. I know it was somewhere in the region where I was born, in the upper part of Las Villas, Zulueta, Remedios, Caibarién, all the villages before you come to the sea. Then the picture of another plantation comes to mind: the Flor de Sagua. I don't know if that was the place where I worked for the first time, but I do remember running away from there once; I decided I'd had enough of that bloody place, and I was off! But they caught me without a struggle, clapped a pair of shackles on me (I can still feel them when I think back), screwed them up tight and sent me back to work wearing them. You talk about this sort of thing today and people don't believe you, but it happened to me and I have to say so.

The owner of that plantation had a funny name, one of those long ones with lots of parts. He was everything

* Little Creole. Creole was a first-generation Cuban, black or white.

bad: stupid, evil-tempered, swollen-headed . . . He used to ride past in the fly with his wife and smart friends through the cane-fields, waving a handkerchief, but that was as near as he ever got to us. The owners never went to the fields. One odd thing about this man: I remember he had a smart Negro, a first-rate driver, with gold rings in his ears and everything. All those drivers were scabs and tale-bearers. You might say they were the dandies of the coloured people.

At the Flor de Sagua I started work on the *bagasse** wagons. I sat on the box and drove the mule. If the wagon was very full I stopped the mule, got down and led it by the rein. The mules were hardmouthed and you had to bear down on the reins like the devil. Your back began to grow hunched. A lot of people are walking around now almost hunchbacked because of those mules. The wagons went out piled to the top. They were always unloaded in the sugar-mill town, and the *bagasse* had to be spread out to dry. It was scattered with a hook, then it was taken, dried, to the furnaces. This was done to make steam. I suppose that was the first work I did. At least, that's what my memory tells me.

All the indoor parts of the plantation were primitive; not like today with their lights and fast machinery. They were called *cachimbos*, because that is the word for a small sugar-mill. In them the sugar was evaporated and drained. There were some which did not make sugar, but syrup and pan sugar. Almost all of them belonged to a single owner; these were called *trapiches*. There were three

* The fibres left after the juice has been extracted from sugar-cane.

sugar-boilers in the *cachimbos*—big copper ones with wide mouths. The first cooked the cane-juice, in the next the froth was taken off, and in the third the treacle was boiled till ready. *Cachaza* was what we called the froth which was left over from the cane-juice. It came off in a hard crust and was very good for pigs. When the treacle was ready, you took a ladle with a long wooden handle and poured it into a trough and from there into the sugar-locker, which stood a short distance from the boilers. That was where they drained the *muscovado*, or unrefined sugar, which had most of the syrup left in it. In those days the centrifuge, as they call it, did not exist.

Once the sugar in the locker had cooled, you had to go in barefoot with spade and shovel and a hand barrow. One Negro always went in front and another behind. The barrow was to take the hogsheads to the *tinglado*, a long shed with two beams where the hogsheads were stacked to drain the sugar. The syrup which drained off the hogsheads was given to the mill-town people and was given to the pigs and sheep. They got very fat on it.

To make refined sugar there were some big funnels into which the raw sugar was poured to be refined. That sugar looked like the sort we have today, white sugar. The funnels were known as 'moulds'.

I know that part of sugar-making better than most people who only know the cane as it is outside, in the fields. And to tell the truth I preferred the inside part, it was easier. At Flor de Sagua I worked in the sugar-locker, but this was after I had got experience working with *bagasse*. That was spade-and-shovel work. To my mind even cane-cutting was preferable. I must have been ten years old then, and that was why they had not sent me to work in the fields. But ten then was like thirty now, because boys worked like oxen.

If a boy was pretty and lively he was sent inside, to the master's house. And there they started softening him up and . . . well, I don't know! They used to give the boy a long palm-leaf and make him stand at one end of the table while they ate. And they said, 'Now see that no flies get in the food!' If a fly did, they scolded him severely and even whipped him. I never did this work because I never wanted to be on closer terms with the masters. I was a runaway from birth.

*

All the slaves lived in barracoons. These dwelling-places no longer exist, so one cannot see them. But I saw them and I never thought well of them. The masters, of course, said they were as clean as new pins. The slaves disliked living under those conditions: being locked up stifled them. The barracoons were large, though some plantations had smaller ones; it depended on the number of slaves in the settlement. Around two hundred slaves of all colours lived in the Flor de Sagua barracoon. This was laid out in rows: two rows facing each other with a door in the middle and a massive padlock to shut the slaves in at night. There were barracoons of wood and barracoons of masonry with tiled roofs. Both types had mud floors and were as dirty as hell. And there was no modern ventilation there! Just a hole in the wall or a

[21]

small barred window. The result was that the place
swarmed with fleas and ticks, which made the inmates
ill with infections and evil spells, for those ticks were
witches. The only way to get rid of them was with hot
wax, and sometimes even that did not work. The masters
wanted the barracoons to look clean outside, so they were
whitewashed. The job was given to the Negroes themselves. The master would say, 'Get some whitewash and
spread it on evenly.' They prepared the whitewash in
large pots inside the barracoons, in the central courtyard.

Horses and goats did not go inside the barracoons, but
there was always some mongrel sniffing about the place
for food. People stayed inside the rooms, which were
small and hot. One says rooms, but they were really
ovens. They had doors with latchkeys to prevent stealing.
You had to be particularly wary of the *criollitos*, who were
born thieving little rascals. They learned to steal like
monkeys.

In the central patio the women washed their own, their
husbands' and their children's clothes in tubs. Those
tubs were not like the ones people use now, they were
much cruder. And they had to be taken first to the river
to swell the wood, because they were made out of fish-
crates, the big ones.

There were no trees either outside or inside the barracoons, just empty solitary spaces. The Negroes could
never get used to this. The Negro likes trees, forests. But
the Chinese! Africa was full of trees, god-trees, banyans,
cedars. But not China—there they have weeds, purslaine,
morning-glory, the sort of thing that creeps along. As the

rooms were so small the slaves relieved themselves in a so-called toilet standing in one corner of the barracoon. Everyone used it. And to wipe your arse afterwards you had to pick leaves and maize husks.

The bell was at the entrance to the mill. The deputy overseer used to ring it. At four-thirty in the morning they rang the Ave Maria—I think there were nine strokes of the bell—and one had to get up immediately. At six they rang another bell called the line-up bell, and everyone had to form up in a place just outside the barracoon, men one side, women the other. Then off to the canefields till eleven, when we ate jerked beef, vegetables and bread. Then, at sunset, came the prayer bell. At half-past eight they rang the last bell for everyone to go to sleep, the silence bell.

The deputy overseer slept inside the barracoon and kept watch. In the mill town there was a white watchman, a Spaniard, to keep an eye on things. Everything was based on watchfulness and the whip. When time passed and the *esquifación*, the slaves' issue of clothing, began to wear out, they would be given a new one. The men's clothes were made of Russian cloth, a coarse linen, sturdy and good for work in the fields—trousers which had large pockets and stood up stiff, a shirt, and a wool cap for the cold. The shoes were generally of rawhide, low-cut with little straps to keep them on. The old men wore sandals, flat-soled with a thong around the big toe. This has always been an African fashion, though white women wear them now and call them mules or slippers. The women were given blouses, skirts and petticoats, and

[23]

if they owned plots of land they bought their own petticoats, white ones, which were prettier and smarter. They
also wore gold rings and earrings. They bought these
trophies from the Turks and Moors who sometimes came
to the barracoons, carrying boxes slung from their
shoulders by a wide leather strap. Lottery-ticket-sellers
also came round, who cheated the Negroes and sold them
all their most expensive tickets. If any of the tickets came
up on the lottery you wouldn't see them for dust. The
guajiros, or white countrymen, also came to barter milk for
jerked beef, or sell it at four cents a bottle. The Negroes
used to buy it because the owners did not provide milk,
and it is necessary because it cures infections and cleans
the system.

These plots of land were the salvation of many slaves,
where they got their real nourishment from. Almost all
of them had their little strips of land to be sown close to
the barracoons, almost behind them. Everything grew
there: sweet potatoes, gourds, okra, kidney beans, which
were like lima beans, yucca and peanuts. They also raised
pigs. And they sold all these products to the whites who
came out from the villages. The Negroes were honest, it
was natural for them to be honest, not knowing much
about things. They sold their goods very cheap. Whole
pigs fetched a doubloon, or a doubloon and a half, in
gold coin, as the money was then, but the blacks didn't
like selling their vegetables. I learned to eat vegetables
from the elders, because they said they were very healthy
food, but during slavery pigs were the mainstay. Pigs gave
more lard then than now, and I think it's because they led

a more natural life. A pig was left to wallow about in the piggeries. The lard cost ten pennies a pound, and the white countrymen came all week long to get their portion. They always paid in silver half-dollars. Later it became quarter-dollars.

Cents were still unknown because they had not crowned Alfonso XIII king as yet, and cents came after his coronation. King Alfonso wanted everything changed, right down to the coinage. Copper money came to Cuba then, worth two cents, if I remember right, and other novelties in the way of money, all due to the King.

Strange as it may seem, the Negroes were able to keep themselves amused in the barracoons. They had their games and pastimes. They played games in the taverns too, but these were different. The favourite game in the barracoons was *tejo*. A split corn-cob was placed on the ground with a coin balanced on top, a line was drawn not far off, and you had to throw a stone from there to hit the cob. If the stone hit the cob so that the coin fell on top of it, the player won the coin, but if it fell nearby, he didn't. This game gave rise to great disputes, and then you had to take a straw to measure whether the coin was nearer the player or the cob.

Tejo was played in the courtyard like skittles, though skittles was not played often, only two or three times altogether that I can remember. Negro coopers used to make the bottle-shaped skittles and wooden balls to play with. This game was open to all comers, and everyone had a go, except the Chinese, who didn't join in much. The balls were rolled along the ground so as to knock down the four or five skittles. It was played just like the modern game they have in the city except that they used to fight over the betting money in those days. The masters didn't like that at all. They forbade certain games, and you had to play those when the overseer was not looking. The overseer was the one who passed on the news and gossip.

The game of *mayombe** was connected with religion. The overseers themselves used to get involved, hoping to benefit. They believed in the witches too, so no one today need be surprised that whites believe in such things. Drumming was part of the *mayombe*. A *nganga*, or large pot, was placed in the centre of the patio. The powers were inside the pot: the saints. People started drumming and singing. They took offerings to the pot and asked for health for themselves and their brothers and peace among themselves. They also made *enkangues*, which were charms of earth from the cemetery; the earth was made into little heaps in four corners, representing the points of the universe. Inside the pot they put a plant called star-shake, together with corn straw to protect the men. When a master punished a slave, the others would collect a little earth and put it in the pot. With the help of this earth they could make the master fall sick or bring some harm upon his family, for so long as the earth was inside the pot the master was imprisoned there and the Devil himself couldn't get him out. This was how the Congolese revenged themselves upon their master.

---

* African word meaning evil spirit; hence name given to the branch of the Stick Cult (see footnote, p. 120) which concentrates on black magic.

The taverns were near the plantations. There were more taverns than ticks in the forest. They were a sort of store where one could buy everything. The slaves themselves used to trade in the taverns, selling the jerkéd beef which they accumulated in the barracoons. They were usually allowed to visit the taverns during the daylight hours and sometimes even in the evenings, but this was not the rule in all the plantations. There was always some master who forbade the slaves to go. The Negroes went to the taverns for brandy. They drank a lot of it to keep their strength up. A glass of good brandy costs half a peso. The owners drank a lot of brandy too, and the quarrels which brewed were no joke. Some of the tavern-keepers were old Spaniards, retired from the army on very little money, five or six pesos' pension.

The taverns were made of wood and palm-bark; no masonry like the modern stores. You had to sit on piled jute sacks or stand. They sold rice, jerked beef, lard and every variety of bean. I knew cases of unscrupulous owners cheating slaves by quoting the wrong prices, and I saw brawls in which a Negro came off worse and was forbidden to return. They noted down anything you bought in a book; when you spent half a peso they made one stroke in the book, and two for a peso. This was the system for buying everything else: round sweet biscuits, salt biscuits, sweets the size of a pea made of different-coloured flours, water-bread and lard. Water-bread cost five cents a stick. It was quite different from the sort you get now. I preferred it. I also remember that they sold sweet cakes, called 'caprices', made of peanut flour and sesame seed. The sesame seed was a Chinese thing; there were Chinese pedlars who went round the plantations selling it, old indentured labourers whose arms were too weak to cut cane and who had taken up peddling.

The taverns were stinking places. A strong smell came from all the goods hanging from the ceiling, sausages, smoked hams, red mortadellas. In spite of this, people used to hold their games there. They spent half their lives at this foolishness. The Negroes were eager to shine at these games. I remember one game they called 'the biscuit', which was played by putting four or five hard salt biscuits on a wooden counter and striking them hard with your prick to see who could break them. Money and drinks were wagered on this game. Whites and blacks played it alike.

Another competition was the jug game. You took a large earthenware jug with a hole in the top and stuck your prick into it. The bottom of the jug was covered with a fine layer of ash, so you could see whether a man had reached the bottom or not when he took it out again.

Then there were other things they played, like cards. It was preferable to play with oil-painted cards, which are the correct ones to play with. There were many types of card games. Some people liked playing with the cards face up, others with them face down, which was a game where you could win a lot of money, but I preferred *monte*, which began in the private houses and then spread to the countryside. *Monte* was played during slavery, in the tavern and in the masters' homes, but I took it up after Abolition. It is very complicated. You have to put two cards on the table and guess which of the two is the highest of the three you still have in your hand. It was always played for money, which is what made it attractive. The banker dealt the cards and the players put on the money. You could win a lot of money, and I won every day. The fact is, *monte* was my weakness; *monte* and women. And with some reason, for you would have had to look hard to find a better player than me. Each card had its name, like now, except that the cards today are not so colourful. In my day they had queens, kings, aces and knaves, and then came all the numbers from two to seven. The cards had pictures on them of men on horseback or wearing crowns, obviously Spaniards, because they never had fellows like that in Cuba, with those lace collars and long hair. They had Indians here in the old days.

Sunday was the liveliest day in the plantations. I don't know where the slaves found the energy for it. Their biggest fiestas were held on that day. On some plantations the drumming started at midday or one o'clock. At Flor de Sagua it began very early. The excitement, the games, and children rushing about started at sunrise. The barracoon came to life in a flash; it was like the end of the world. And in spite of work and everything the people woke up cheerful. The overseer and deputy overseer came into the barracoon and started chatting up the black women. I noticed that the Chinese kept apart; those buggers had no ear for drums and they stayed in their little corners. But they thought a lot; to my mind they spent more time thinking than the blacks. No one took any notice of them, and people went on with their dances.

The one I remember best is the *yuka*. Three drums were played for the *yuka*: the *caja*, the *mula*, and the *cachimbo*, which was the smallest one. In the background they drummed with two sticks on hollowed-out cedar trunks. The slaves made those themselves, and I think they were called *catá*. The *yuka* was danced in couples, with wild movements. Sometimes they swooped about like birds, and it almost looked as if they were going to fly, they moved so fast. They gave little hops with their hands on their waists. Everyone sang to excite the dancers.

There was another more complicated dance. I don't know whether it was really a dance or a game, because they punched each other really hard. This dance they called the *mani* or peanut dance. The dancers formed a circle of forty or fifty men, and they started hitting each other. Whoever got hit went in to dance. They wore ordinary work clothes, with coloured print scarves round their heads and at their waists. (These scarves were used to bundle up the slaves' clothing and take it to the wash: they were called *vayajá* scarves.) The men used to weight their fists with magic charms to make the *mani* blows more effective. The women didn't dance but stood round in a chorus, clapping, and they used to scream with fright, for often a Negro fell and failed to get up again. *Mani* was a cruel game. The dancers did not make bets on the outcome. On some plantations the masters themselves made bets, but I don't remember this happening at Flor

de Sagua. What they did was to forbid slaves to hit each
other so hard, because sometimes they were too bruised
to work. The boys could not take part, but they watched
and took it all in. I haven't forgotten a thing myself.

As soon as the drums started on Sunday the Negroes
went down to the stream to bathe—there was always a
little stream near every plantation. It sometimes happened
that a woman lingered behind and met a man just as he
was about to go into the water. Then they would go off
together and get down to business. If not, they would go
to the reservoirs, which were the pools they dug to
store water. They also used to play hide-and-seek there,
chasing the women and trying to catch them.

The women who were not involved in this little game
stayed in the barracoons and washed themselves in a
tub. These tubs were very big and there were one or
two for the whole settlement.

Shaving and cutting hair was done by the slaves themselves. They took a long knife and, like someone groom-
ing a horse, they sliced off the woolly hair. There was
always someone who liked to clip, and he became the
expert. They cut hair the way they do now. And it never
hurt, because hair is the most peculiar stuff; although
you can see it growing and everything, it's dead. The
women arranged their hair with curls and little partings.
Their heads used to look like melon skins. They liked the
excitement of fixing their hair one way one day and
another way the next. One day it would have little partings, the next day ringlets, another day it would be
combed flat. They cleaned their teeth with strips of

soap-tree bark, and this made them very white. All this excitement was reserved for Sundays.

Everyone had a special outfit that day. The Negroes bought themselves rawhide boots, in a style I haven't seen since, from nearby shops where they went with the master's permission. They wore red and green *vayajá* scarves around their necks, and round their heads and waists too, like in the *maní* dance. And they decked themselves with rings in their ears and rings on all their fingers, real gold. Some of them wore not gold but fine silver bracelets which came as high as their elbows, and patent leather shoes.

The slaves of French descent danced in pairs, not touching, circling slowly around. If one of them danced outstandingly well they tied silk scarves of all colours to his knees as a prize. They sang in patois and played two big drums with their hands. This was called the French dance.

I remember one instrument called a *marímbula*, which was very small. It was made of wickerwork and sounded as loud as a drum and had a little hole for the voice to come out of. They used this to accompany the Congo drums, and possibly the French too, but I can't be sure. The *marímbulas* made a very strange noise, and lots of people, particularly the *guajiros**, didn't like them because they said they sounded like voices from another world.

As I recall, their own music at that time was made with the guitar only. Later, in the Nineties, they played

* Peasants, originally white settlers, but by this time black and Mulatto also.

*danzónes** on pianolas, with accordions and gourds. But
the white man has always had a very different music
from the black man. White man's music is without the
drumming and is more insipid.

More or less the same goes for religion. The African
gods are different, though they resemble the others, the
priests' gods. They are more powerful and less adorned.
Right now if you were to go to a Catholic church you
would not see apples, stones or cock's feathers. But this
is the first thing you see in an African house. The African
is cruder.

I knew of two African religions in the barracoons:
the Lucumi and the Congolese. The Congolese was the
more important. It was well known at the Flor de Sagua
because their magic-men used to put spells on people
and get possession of them, and their practice of sooth-
saying won them the confidence of all the slaves. I got
to know the elders of both religions after Abolition.

I remember the *Chicherekú†* at Flor de Sagua. The
Chicherekú was a Congolese by birth who did not speak
Spanish. He was a little man with a big head who used to
run about the barracoons and jump upon you from
behind. I often saw him and heard him squealing like a
rat. This is true. Until recently in Porfuerza there was a
man who ran about in the same way. People used to
run away from him because they said he was the Devil
himself and he was bound up with *mayombe* and death.
You dared not play with the *Chicherekú* because it could

* *Danzón:* a slow, stately Cuban dance popular in the last century.
† African word for bogey-man.

be dangerous. Personally I don't much like talking of of him, because I have never laid eyes on him again, and if by some chance . . . Well, these things are the Devil's own!

The Congolese used the dead and snakes for their religious rites. They called the dead *nkise* and the snakes *emboba*. They prepared big pots called *ngangas* which would walk about and all, and that was where the secret of their spells lay. All the Congolese had these pots for *mayombe*. The *ngangas* had to work with the sun, because the sun has always been the strength and wisdom of men, as the moon is of women. But the sun is more important because it is he who gives life to the moon. The Congolese worked magic with the sun almost every day. When they had trouble with a particular person they would follow him along a path, collect up some of the dust he walked upon and put it in the *nganga* or in some little secret place. As the sun went down that person's life would begin to ebb away, and at sunset he would be dying. I mention this because it is something I often saw under slavery.

If you think about it, the Congolese were murderers, although they only killed people who were harming them. No one ever tried to put a spell on me because I have always kept apart and not meddled in other people's affairs.

The Congolese were more involved with witchcraft than the Lucumi, who had more to do with the saints and with God. The Lucumi liked rising early with the strength of the morning and looking up into the sky and

saying prayers and sprinkling water on the ground. The
Lucumi were at it when you least expected it. I have
seen old Negroes kneel on the ground for more than three
hours at a time, speaking in their own tongue and
prophesying. The difference between the Congolese
and the Lucumi was that the former solved problems
while the latter told the future. This they did with *dilog-
gunes*, which are round, white shells from Africa with
mystery inside. The god Eleggua's* eyes are made from
this shell.

The old Lucumis would shut themselves up in rooms
in the barracoon and they could rid you of even the
wickedness you were doing. If a Negro lusted after a
woman, the Lucumis would calm him. I think they did
this with coconut shells, *obi*, which were sacred. They
were the same as the coconuts today, which are still
sacred and may not be touched. If a man defiled a
coconut, a great punishment befell him. I knew when
things went well, because the coconut said so. He would
command *Alafia*,† to be said so that people would
know that all was well. The saints spoke through the
coconuts and the chief of these was Obatalá, who was
an old man, they said, and only wore white. They also
said it was Obatalá who made you and I don't know
what else, but it is from Nature one comes, and this is
true of Obatalá too.

* Elegguá, Obatalá, Changó, Yemaya: gods of the Yoruba, a Nigerian
tribe, worshipped in Cuba by the followers of *santeria*, see footnote on
p. 80.

† Lucumi expression meaning 'all goes well', used particularly in
the system of divination with sacred coconuts.

The old Lucumis liked to have their wooden figures of the gods with them in the barracoon. All these figures had big heads and were called *oché*. Elegguá was made of cement, but Changó and Yemaya were of wood, made by the carpenters themselves.

They made the saints' marks on the walls of their rooms with charcoal and white chalk, long lines and circles, each one standing for a saint, but they said that they were secrets. These blacks made a secret of everything. They have changed a lot now, but in those days the hardest thing you could do was to try to win the confidence of one of them.

The other religion was the Catholic one. This was introduced by the priests, but nothing in the world would induce them to enter the slaves' quarters. They were fastidious people, with a solemn air which did not fit the barracoons—so solemn that there were Negroes who took everything they said literally. This had a bad effect on them. They read the catechism and read it to the others with all the words and prayers. Those Negroes who were household slaves came as messengers of the priests and got together with the others, the field slaves, in the sugar-mill towns. The fact is I never learned that doctrine because I did not understand a thing about it. I don't think the household slaves did either, although, being so refined and well-treated, they all made out they were Christian. The household slaves were given rewards by the masters, and I never saw one of them badly punished. When they were ordered to go to the fields to cut cane or tend the pigs, they would pretend to be ill so they needn't work. For this reason the field slaves could not stand the sight of them. The household slaves sometimes came to the barracoons to visit relations and used to take back fruit and vegetables for the master's house; I don't know whether the slaves made them presents from their plots of land or whether they just took them. They caused a lot of trouble in the barracoons. The men came and tried to take liberties with the women. That was the source of the worst tensions. I was about twelve then, and I saw the whole rumpus.

There were other tensions. For instance, there was no love lost between the Congolese magic-men and the Congolese Christians, each of whom thought they were good and the others wicked. This still goes on in Cuba. The Lucumi and Congolese did not get on either; it went back to the difference between saints and witchcraft. The only ones who had no problems were the old men born in Africa. They were special people and had to be treated differently because they knew all religious matters.

Many brawls were avoided because the masters changed the slaves around. They kept them divided among themselves to prevent a rash of escapes. That was why the slaves of different plantations never got together with each other.

The Lucumis didn't like cutting cane, and many of them ran away. They were the most rebellious and courageous slaves. Not so the Congolese; they were cowardly as a rule, but strong workers who worked hard without complaining. There is a common rat called Congolese, and very cowardly it is too.

In the plantations there were Negroes from different countries, all different physically. The Congolese were black-skinned, though there were many of mixed blood with yellowish skins and light hair. They were usually small. The Mandingas were reddish-skinned, tall and very strong. I swear by my mother they were a bunch of crooks, too! They kept apart from the rest. The Gangas were nice people, rather short and freckled. Many of them became runaways. The Carabalís were like the Musungo Congolese, uncivilised brutes. They only killed pigs on Sundays and at Easter and, being good businessmen, they killed them to sell, not to eat themselves. From this comes a saying, 'Clever Carabalí, kills pig on Sunday,' I got to know all these people better after slavery was abolished.

*

All the plantations had an infirmary near the barracoon, a big wooden hut where they took the pregnant women. You were born there and stayed there till you were six or seven, when you went to live in the barracoons and began work, like the rest. There were Negro wet-nurses and cooks there to look after the *criollitos* and feed them. If anyone was injured in the fields or fell ill, these women would doctor him with herbs and brews. They could cure anything. Sometimes a *criollito* never saw his parents again because the boss moved them to another plantation, and so the wet-nurses would be in sole charge of the child. But who wants to bother with another person's child? They used to bath the children and cut their hair in the infirmaries too. A child of good stock cost five hundred pesos, that is the child of strong, tall parents. Tall Negroes were privileged. The masters picked them out to mate them with tall, healthy women and shut them up together in the barracoon and forced them to sleep together. The women had to produce healthy babies every year. I tell you, it was like breeding animals. Well, if the Negress didn't produce as expected, the couple were separated and she was sent to work in the fields again. Women who were barren were unlucky because they had to go back to being beasts of burden again, but they were allowed to choose their own husbands. It often happened that a women would be chasing one man with twenty more after her. The magic-men would settle these problems with their potions.

If you went to a magic-man to ask his help in getting a woman, he would tell you to get hold of a shred of her tobacco, if she smoked. This was ground together with a Cantharis fly, one of the green harmful ones, into a powder which you gave to the woman in water. That was the way to seduce them. Another spell consisted of grinding up a hummingbird's heart to powder and giving this to a woman in her tobacco. If you merely wanted to make fun of a woman, you only had to send for some snuff from the apothecary's. This was enough to make any woman die of shame. You put it in a place where they used to sit down, and if only a little touched their bums they started farting. It was something to see those women with cosmetics all over their faces farting about the place!

The old Negroes were entertained by these carryings-on. When they were over sixty they stopped working in the fields. Not that any of them ever knew their ages exactly. What happened was that when a man grew weak and stayed huddled in a corner, the overseers would make him a doorkeeper or watchman stationed at the gate of the barracoon or outside the pigsties, or he would be sent to help the women in the kitchen. Some of the old men had their little plots of ground and passed their time working in them. Doing this sort of job gave them time for witchcraft. They were not punished or taken much notice of, but they had to be quiet and obedient. That much was expected.

I saw many horrors in the way of punishment under slavery. That was why I didn't like the life. The stocks, which were in the boiler-house, were the cruellest. Some were for standing and others for lying down. They were made of thick planks with holes for the head, hands and feet. They would keep slaves fastened up like this for two or three months for some trivial offence. They whipped the pregnant women too, but lying face down with a hollow in the ground for their bellies. They whipped them hard, but they took good care not to damage the babies because they wanted as many of those as possible. The most common punishment was flogging; this was given by the overseer with a rawhide lash which made weals on the skin. They also had whips made of the fibres of some jungle plant which stung like the devil and flayed the skin off in strips. I saw many handsome big Negroes with raw backs. Afterwards the cuts were covered with compresses of tobacco leaves, urine and salt.

Life was hard and bodies wore out. Anyone who did

not take to the hills as a runaway when he was young had
to become a slave. It was preferable to be on your own
on the loose than locked up in all that dirt and rottenness.
In any event, life tended to be solitary because there were
none too many women around. To have one of your
own you had either to be over twenty-five or catch
yourself one in the fields. The old men did not want
the youths to have women. They said a man should
wait until he was twenty-five to have experiences. Some
men did not suffer much, being used to this life. Others
had sex between themselves and did not want to know
anything of women. This was their life—sodomy. The
effeminate men washed the clothes and did the cooking
too, if they had a 'husband'. They were good workers and
occupied themselves with their plots of land, giving the
produce to their 'husbands' to sell to the white farmers.
It was after Abolition that the term 'effeminate' came into
use, for the practice persisted. I don't think it can have
come from Africa, because the old men hated it. They
would have nothing to do with queers. To tell the truth,
it never bothered me. I am of the opinion that a man can
stick his arse where he wants.

*

Everyone wearied of the life, and the ones who got
used to it were broken in spirit. Life in the forest was
healthier. You caught lots of illnesses in the barracoons,
in fact men got sicker there than anywhere else. It was
not unusual to find a Negro with as many as three
sicknesses at once. If it wasn't colic it was whooping

cough. Colic gave you a pain in the gut which lasted a few hours and left you shagged. Whooping cough and measles were catching. But the worst sicknesses, which made a skeleton of everyone, were smallpox and the black sickness. Smallpox left men all swollen, and the black sickness took them by surprise; it struck suddenly and between one bout of vomiting and the next you ended up a corpse. There was one type of sickness the whites picked up, a sickness of the veins and male organs. It could only be got rid of with black women; if the man who had it slept with a Negress he was cured immediately.

There were no powerful medicines in those days and no doctors to be found anywhere. It was the nurses who were half witches who cured people with their home-made remedies. They often cured illnesses the doctors couldn't understand. The solution doesn't lie in feeling you and pinching your tongue; the secret is to trust the plants and herbs, which are the mother of medicine. Africans from the other side, across the sea, are never sick because they have the necessary plants at hand.

If a slave caught an infectious disease, they would take him from his room and move him to the infirmary and try to cure him. If he died they put him in a big box and carried him off to the cemetery. The overseer usually came and gave instructions to the settlement to bury him. He would say, 'We are going to bury this Negro who has done his time.' And the slaves hurried along there, for when someone died everyone mourned.

The cemetery was in the plantation itself, about a hundred yards from the barracoon. To bury slaves, they dug a hole in the ground, filled it in and stuck a cross on top to keep away enemies and the Devil. Now they call it a crucifix. If anyone wears a cross around his neck it is because someone has tried to harm him.

Once they buried a Congolese and he raised his head. He was still alive. I was told this story in Santo Domingo, after Abolition. The whole district of Jicotea knows of it. It happened on a small plantation called El Diamante which belonged to Marinello's father, the one who talks a lot about Martí.* Everyone took fright and ran away. A few days later the Congolese appeared in the barra-coon; they say he entered very slowly so as not to scare everyone, but when people saw him they took fright again. When the overseer asked what had happened, he said, 'They put me in a hole because of my cholera and when I was cured I came out.' After that, whenever anyone caught cholera or another disease, they left him for days and days in the coffin until he grew as cold as ice.

These stories are true, but one I am convinced is a fabrication because I never saw such a thing, and that is that some Negroes committed suicide. Before, when the Indians were in Cuba, suicide did happen. They did not want to become Christians, and they hanged themselves from trees. But the Negroes did not do that, they escaped by flying. They flew through the sky and returned to their own lands. The Musundi Congolese were the ones

* Martí, often known as the 'Apostle' or 'the Father of Cuba', was the leader of Cuba's national War of Independence and also a poet and essayist of great influence in the Spanish-speaking world. Juan Marinello, one of Cuba's leading Communists, is an important critic of Martí's literary work.

that flew the most; they disappeared by means of witch-craft. They did the same as the Canary Island witches, but without making a sound. There are those who say the Negroes threw themselves into rivers. This is untrue. The truth is they fastened a chain to their waists which was full of magic. That was where their power came from. I know all this intimately, and it is true beyond a doubt.

The Chinese did not fly, nor did they want to go back to their own country, but they did commit suicide. They did it silently. After several days they would turn up hanging from a tree or dead on the ground. They did everything in silence. They used to kill the very overseers themselves with sticks or knives. The Chinese respected no one. They were born rebels. Often the master would appoint an overseer of their own race so that he might win their trust. Then they did not kill him. When slavery ended I met other Chinese in Sagua la Grande, but they were different and very civilised.

Life in the Forest

═══════════

I HAVE never forgotten the first time I tried to escape. That time I failed, and I stayed a slave for several years longer from fear of having the shackles put on me again. But I had the spirit of a runaway watching over me, which never left me. And I kept my plans to myself so that no one could give me away. I thought of nothing else; the idea went round and round my head and would not leave me in peace; nothing could get rid of it, at times it almost tormented me. The old Negroes did not care for escaping, the women still less. There were few runaways. People were afraid of the forest. They said anyone who ran away was bound to be recaptured. But I gave more thought to this idea than the others did. I always had the feeling that I would like the forest and I knew that it was hell working in the fields, for you couldn't do anything for yourself. Everything went by what the master said.

One day I began to keep my eye on the overseer. I had already been sizing him up for some time. That son-of-a-bitch obsessed me, and nothing could make me forget him. I think he was Spanish. I remember that he was tall and never took his hat off. All the blacks respected

him because he would take the skin off your back with a
single stroke of his whip. The fact is I was hot-headed
that day. I don't know what came over me, but I was
filled with a rage which burned me up just to look at the
man.

I whistled at him from a distance, and he looked round
and then turned his back; that was when I picked up a
stone and threw it at his head. I know it must have hit
him because he shouted to the others to seize me. But
that was the last he saw of me, because I took to the forest
there and then.

I spent several days walking about in no particular
direction. I had never left the plantation before. I walked
uphill, downhill, in every direction. I know I got to a
farm near the Siguanea, where I was forced to rest. My
feet were blistered and my hands were swollen and
festering. I camped under a tree. I made myself a shelter
of banana-leaves in a few hours and I stayed there four or
five days. I only had to hear the sound of a human voice
to be off like a bullet. It was a terrible thing to be captured
again after you had run away.

Then I had the idea of hiding in a cave. I lived there
for something like a year and a half. The reason I chose
it was that I thought it might save me wandering about
so much and also that all the pigs in the district, from the
farms and smallholdings and allotments, used to come to
a sort of marsh near the mouth of the cave to bathe and
wallow in the water. I caught them very easily because
they came up one behind the other. I used to cook myself up a pig every week. This cave of mine was very big

and as black as a wolf's mouth. Its name was Guajabán,
near the village of Remedios. It was very dangerous
because there was no other way out; you had to enter
and leave by the mouth. I was very curious to find
another exit, but I preferred to stay in the mouth of the
cave with the *majases* which are very dangerous snakes.*
They knock a person down with their breath, a snake
breath you cannot feel, and then they put you to sleep
to suck your blood. That was why I was always on guard
and lit a fire to frighten them off. Anyone who dozes off
in a cave is in a bad way. I did not want to see a snake
even from a distance. The Congolese, and this is a fact,
told me that the *majases* lived for over a thousand years,
and when they got to a thousand they turned into marine
creatures and went off to live in the sea like any other fish.

The cave was like a house inside, only a little darker,
as you would expect. Ah, and the stink! Yes, it stank of
bat droppings! I used to walk about on them because
they were as soft as a feather bed. The bats lead a free
life in caves. They were and are the masters of caves.
It is the same everywhere in the world. As no one kills
them they live for scores of years, though not as long as
the *majases*. Their droppings turn to dust and are thrown
on the ground to make pasture for animals and to fertilise
crops.

Once I almost set fire to the place. I struck a spark and
flames leapt through the cave. It was because of the bat
droppings. After Abolition I told a Congolese the story
of how I lived with the bats, and the liar—the Congolese

* In fact they are harmless.

were even worse than you could imagine—said, 'A Creole like you doesn't know a thing. In my country what you call a bat is as big as a pigeon.' I knew this was untrue. They fooled half the world with their tales. But I just listened and was inwardly amused.

The cave was silent. The only sound was the bats going 'Chui, chui, chui'. They didn't know how to sing, but they spoke to each other, they understood each other. I noticed that one of them would go 'Chui, chui, chui' and the whole band would follow him wherever he went. They were very united in everything. Bats don't have wings. They are nothing but a scrap of black rag with a little black head, very dark and ugly, and if you look closely at them they are like mice. In that cave I was, as it were, just summering. What I really liked was the forest, and after a year and a half I left that dark place and took to the forest tracks. I went into the Siguanea forests again and spent a long time there. I cared for myself as if I were a pampered child. I didn't want to be taken into slavery again. It was repugnant to me, it was shameful. I have always felt like that about slavery. It was like a plague—it still seems like that today.

I was careful about making sounds or showing lights. If I left a trail they would follow me and catch me. I walked up and down so many hills that my arms and legs became as hard as wood. I came to know the forest gradually, and I began to like it. Sometimes I forgot I was a runaway and started whistling. I used to whistle to dispel the fear of the first days. They say whistling drives away evil spirits. But in the forest a runaway had to be on his guard, and I stopped in case the *ranchadores* came after me. To track down runaway slaves, the masters used to send for a posse of *ranchadores*, brutal white countrymen with hunting dogs which would drag you out of the forest with their teeth. I never ran into any of them or even saw one close up. They were trained to catch Negroes; if one of them saw a Negro he would give chase. If I happened to hear barking nearby I would take off my clothes immediately, because once you are naked the dogs can't smell anything. Now I see a dog and it doesn't mean a thing, but if I had seen one then you wouldn't have seen my heels for miles around. I have never felt drawn to dogs. To my mind they have wicked instincts.

When a *ranchador* caught a slave, the master would give him money, a gold onza or more. In those days an onza was worth seventeen pesos. There's no knowing how many white countrymen were involved in that business!

To tell the truth, I lived very well as a runaway, hidden but comfortable. I did not let the other runaways catch sight of me: 'Runaway meets runaway, sells runaway.' There were many things I didn't do. For a long time I didn't speak to a soul. I liked this solitude. The other runaways always stayed in groups of twos and threes, but this was dangerous because when it rained their footprints showed up in the mud, and lots of idiots were caught that way.

*

There were some freed slaves around. I saw them going

[49]

into the forest to look for herbs and *jutías*, edible rats. I never spoke to them or went near them, in fact I took good care to hide from them. Some of them worked on the land, and as soon as they left the coast clear, I took advantage of their absence to steal their vegetables and pigs. Most of them raised pigs on their plots of land. But I preferred to steal from the smallholdings because there was more of everything and it was easier. The smallholdings were bigger than the plots, far bigger, almost like big farms. The Negroes didn't have such luxuries. Those *guajíros* really lived very well in their palm-bark houses. I used to watch them at their music-making from a safe distance. Sometimes I could even hear them. They played small accordions, kettledrums, gourds, maraccas and calabashes. Those were their favourite instruments. I didn't learn their names till after I left the forest because, as a runaway, I was ignorant of everything.

They enjoyed dancing. But they didn't dance to the black man's music. They liked the *zapateo* and the *caringa*.* They all used to get together to dance the *zapateo* in the evenings, around five o'clock. The men wore coloured scarves around their necks and the women wore them around their heads. If one man excelled in the dance, his woman would come up and put a hat on top of the one he was wearing. This was the prize. I watched it all from a safe distance, taking it all in. I even saw them playing their pianolas. They played every

* Folk dances popular in the nineteenth century, especially among white country people. The *caringa* was of African origin and usually took the form of a scurrilous song accompanied by a dance.

sort of instrument there. They made a lot of noise, but it was as pretty as could be. From time to time one of the men would grab a gourd to accompany the pianola. The pianolas played the music that was popular at the time, the *danzón*.

On Sundays the *guajíros* wore white and their women put flowers on their heads and wore their hair loose, then they joined the rest of the festive company and got together in the taverns to celebrate. The men liked linen and drill. They made themselves long shirts like jackets, with big pockets. The *guajíros* in those days lived better than people realise. They got tips from the masters almost every day. Naturally the two got along very well and did their dirty work together. But in my view the runaway lived better than the *guajíro*; he had greater freedom.

I had to forage for food for a long time, but there was always enough. 'The careful tortoise carries his house on his back.' I liked vegetables and beans and pork best. I think it is because of the pork that I have lived so long. I used to eat it every day, and it never disagreed with me. I would creep up to the smallholdings at night to catch piglets, taking care that no one heard me. I grabbed the first one I saw by the neck, clapped a halter round it, slung it over my shoulder and started to run, keeping my hand over its snout to stop it squealing. When I reached my camp I set it down and looked it over. If it was well fed and weighed twenty pounds or so, I had meals for a fortnight.

I led a half-wild existence as a runaway. I hunted

animals like *jutías*. The *jutía* runs like the devil, and you need wings on your feet to catch it. I was very fond of smoked *jutía*. I don't know what people think of it today, but they never eat it. I used to catch one and smoke it without salt, and it lasted me months. The *jutía* is the healthiest food there is, though vegetables are better for the bones. The man who eats vegetables daily, particularly malanga roots, has no trouble from his bones. There are plenty of these wild vegetables in the forest. The malanga has a big leaf which shines at night. You can recognise it at once.

All the forest leaves have their uses. The leaves of tobacco plants and mulberry-trees cure stings. If I saw some insect bite was festering, I picked a tobacco leaf and chewed it thoroughly, then I laid it on the sting and the swelling went. Often, when it was cold, my bones would ache, a dry pain which would not go away. Then I made myself an infusion of rosemary leaves to soothe it, and it was cured at once. The cold also gave me bad coughs. When I got catarrh and a cough, I would pick this big leaf and lay it on my chest. I never knew its name, but it gave out a whitish liquid which was very warming; that soothed my cough. When I caught a cold, my eyes used to itch maddeningly, and the same used to happen as a result of the sun; in that case I laid a few leaves of the *ítamo* plant out to catch the dew overnight, and the next day I washed my eyes carefully with them. *Ítamo* is the best thing for this. The stuff they sell in pharmacies today is *ítamo*, but what happens is that they put it into little bottles and it looks like something else. As one grows older this eye trouble disappears. I have not had any itching bouts for years now.

The macaw-tree leaf provided me with smokes. I made tight-rolled neat little cigarettes with it. Tobacco was one of my relaxations. After I left the forest I stopped smoking tobacco, but while I was a runaway I smoked all the time.

And I drank coffee which I made with roast *guanina* leaves. I had to grind the leaves with the bottom of a bottle. When the mixture was ground right down, I filtered it and there was my coffee. I could always add a little wild honey to give it flavour. Coffee with honey strengthens the organism. You were always fit and strong in the forest.

Townsfolk are feeble because they are mad about lard. I have never liked lard because it weakens the body. The person who eats a lot of it grows fat and sluggish. Lard is bad for the circulation and it strangles people. Bees' honey is one of the best things there is for health. It was easy to get in the forest. I used to find it in the hollows of hardwood trees. I used it to make *chanchanchara*, a delicious drink made of stream-water and honey, and best drunk cold. It was better for you than any modern medicine; it was natural. When there was no stream nearby I hunted around till I found a spring. In the forest there are springs of sweet water—the coldest and clearest I have seen in my life—which run down-hill.

The truth is I lacked for nothing in the forest. The only thing I could not manage was sex. Since there were no women around I had to keep the appetite in check. It wasn't even possible to fuck a mare because they whinnied like demons, and if the white countrymen had heard the din they would have come rushing out immediately. I was not going to have anyone clap me in irons for a mare.

I was never short of fire. During my first few days in the forest I had matches. Then they ran out, and I had to use my *yesca*, a black ash that I kept in one of the tinderboxes the Spaniards sold in taverns. It was easy to get a fire going. All you had to do was rub a stone on the tinderbox till it sparked. I learned this from the Canary Islanders while I was a slave. I never liked them as they were domineering and petty. The Galicians were nicer and got on better with the Negroes.

As I have always liked being my own man, I kept well away from everyone. I even kept away from the insects. To frighten off snakes I fired a big log and left it burning all night. They did not come near because they thought the log was a devil or an enemy of theirs. That's why I say I enjoyed my life as a runaway. I looked after myself, and I protected myself too. I used knives and half-sized machetes made by the firm of Collins, which were the ones used by the rural police, to clear the undergrowth and hunt animals, and I kept them ready in case a *ranchador* tried to take me by surprise—though that would have been difficult, as I kept on the move. I walked so much in the sun that at times my head began to burn and become, I imagined, quite red. Then I would be seized with a strong fever which I got rid of by wrap-

ping myself up a bit or putting fresh leaves on my forehead,
plantain as a rule. The problem was that I had no hat.
I used to imagine the heat must be getting into my head
and softening my brain.

When the fever passed, and it sometimes lasted several
days, I dipped myself in the first river I came across and
came out like new. The river water did me no harm. I
think river water is the best thing for health, because it's
so cold. This is good, because it hardens you. The bones
feel firm. The rain used to give me a touch of catarrh
which I cured with a brew of *cuajaní* berries and bees'
honey. So as not to get wet I sheltered myself with palm-
leaves, piling them on top of a frame made of four forked
sticks to make a hut. These huts were often seen after
slavery and during the war. They looked like Indian
shacks.

I spent most of the time walking or sleeping. At midday and at five in the afternoon I could hear the *fotuto*,*
which the women blew to call their husbands home. It
sounded like this: 'Fuuuu, fu, fu, fu, fu.' At night I
slept at my ease. That was why I got so fat. I never
thought about anything. My life was all eating, sleeping
and keeping watch. I liked going to the hills at night,
they were quieter and safer. *Ranchadores* and wild
animals found difficulty in getting there. I went as far
as Trinidad. From the top of those hills you could see
the town and the sea.

The nearer I got to the coast the bigger the sea got. I
always imagined the sea like an immense river. Some-

---

* A large conch used as a trumpet in the country districts.

times I stared hard at it and it went the strangest white colour and was swallowed up in my eyes. The sea is another great mystery of Nature, and it is very important, because it can take men and close over them and never give them up. Those are what they call shipwrecked men.

One thing I remember really clearly is the forest birds. They are something I cannot forget. I remember them all. Some were pretty and some were hellishly ugly. They frightened me a lot at first, but then I got used to hearing them. I even got so I felt they were taking care of me. The *cotunto* was a real bastard. It was a black, *black* bird, which said, 'You, you, you, you, you, you, you ate the cheese up.' And it kept on saying this till I answered, 'Get away!' and it went. I heard it crystal clear. There was another bird which used to answer it as well; it went, 'Cu, cu, cu, cu, cu, cu,' and sounded like a ghost.

The *sijú* was one of the birds which tormented me most. It always came at night. That creature was the ugliest thing in the forest! It had white feet and yellow eyes. It shrieked out something like this: 'Cus, cus, cuuuus.'

The barn-owl had a sad song, but then it was a witch. It looked for dead mice. It cried, 'Chua, chua, chua, kui, kui,' and flew off like a ray of light. When I saw a barn-owl in my path, especially when it was flying to and fro, I used to take a different way because I knew it was warning me of an enemy nearby, or death itself. The barn-owl is wise and strange. I recollect that the witches had a great respect for her and worked magic with her, the *sunsundamba*, as she is called in Africa. The barn-owl may well have left Cuba. I have never seen one again. Those birds go from country to country.

The sparrow came here from Spain and has founded an immense tribe here. Also the *tocororo*, which is half a greenish colour. It wears a scarlet sash across its breast, just like one the King of Spain has. The overseers used to say that it was a messenger from the King. I know it was forbidden even to look at a *tocororo*. The Negro who killed one was killing the King. I saw lots of men get the lash for killing sparrows and *tocororo*. I liked the *tocororo* because it sang as if it was hopping about, like this: 'Có, co, có, co, có, co.'

A bird which was a real son-of-a-bitch was the *ciguapa*. It whistled just like a man and it froze the soul to hear it. I don't like to think how often those creatures upset me.

*

I got used to living with trees in the forest. They have their noises too, because the leaves hiss in the air. There is one tree with a big white leaf which looks like a bird at night. I could swear that tree spoke. It went, 'Uch, uch, uch, ui, ui, ui, uch, uch.' Trees also cast shadows which do no harm, although one should not walk on them at night. I think trees' shadows must be like men's spirits. The spirit is the reflection of the soul, this is clear.

One thing it is not given to us men to see is the soul.

We cannot say whether it is of such or such a colour. The soul is one of the greatest things in the world. Dreams are there to put us in touch with it. The Congolese elders used to say that the soul was like a witchcraft inside you and that there were good spirits and bad spirits, or rather, good souls and bad souls, and that everybody had them. As far as I can see, some people only have the magic sort of souls, while others have ordinary ones. But the ordinary ones are better, I think, because the others are in league with the Devil. It can happen that the soul leaves the body—when a person dies or sleeps—and joins the other souls wandering in space. It does this to rest itself, because so much strife at all times would be unbearable. There are people who don't like being called while they are asleep, because they are easily frightened and could die suddenly. This is because the soul travels far away during sleep and leaves the body empty. I sometimes get the shivers at night, and the same used to happen in the forest. Then I cover myself well because this is God's warning to one to take care of oneself. People who get the shivers need to pray a lot.

The heart is very different. It never leaves its post. If you put your hand on your left side you can make sure that it is beating. But the day it stops no one can help but go stiff. That is why you should not trust it.

Now the most important thing of all is the guardian angel. It is he who makes you go forwards or back. To my mind, the angel ranks higher than the soul or heart. He is always at your feet, watching over you and seeing everything. Nothing will ever make him go. I have thought a lot about these things, and I still find them a bit obscure. These are the thoughts which come when one is alone. Man is thinking at all times. Even when he dreams, it is as though he were thinking. It is not good to speak of these thoughts. There is danger of decadence setting in. You cannot put much trust in people. How many people ask you questions so as to be able to use the information against you afterwards! Besides, this business of the spirits is infinite, like debts which keep piling up. No one knows the end. The truth is I don't even trust the Holy Ghost. That was why I stayed on my own as a runaway. I did nothing except listen to the birds and trees, and eat, but I never spoke to a soul. I remember I was so hairy my whiskers hung in ringlets. It was a sight to inspire fear. When I came out of the forest and went into the villages an old man called Ta Migue cropped me with a big pair of scissors. He gave me such a close crop I looked like a thoroughbred. I felt strange with all that wool gone, tremendously cold. The hair started growing again in a few days. Negroes have this tendency—I have never seen a bald Negro, not one. It was the Galicians who brought baldness to Cuba.

All my life I have liked the forest, but when slavery ended I stopped being a runaway. I realised from the way the people were cheering and shouting that slavery had ended, and so I came out of the forest. They were shouting, 'We're free now.' But I didn't join in, I thought it might be a lie. I don't know . . . anyway, I went up to a plantation and let my head appear little by little till I was out in the open. That was while Martinez Campos was Governor, the slaves said it was he who had freed them. All the same, years passed and there were still slaves in Cuba. It lasted longer than people think.

When I left the forest and began walking, I met an old woman carrying two children in her arms. I called to her, and when she came up I asked her, 'Tell me, is it true we are no longer slaves?' She replied, 'No, son, we are free now.' I went on walking the way I was going and began to look for work. Lots of Negroes wanted to be friends with me, and they used to ask me what I had done as a runaway. I told them, 'Nothing.' I have always been one for my independence. Idle gossip never helped anyone. I went for years and years without talking to anyone at all.

PART II

ABOLITION

————

Life in the Plantations

AFTER all this time in the forest I had become half savage. I didn't want to work anywhere, and I was afraid they would shut me up again. I knew quite well that slavery had not ended completely. A lot of people asked me what I was doing and where I came from. Sometimes I told them, 'My name is Stephen and I was a runaway slave.' Other times I said I had been working on a certain plantation and could not find my relations. I must have been about twenty at the time. This was before I came across my relations. That happened later.

Since I did not know anyone I walked from village to village for several months. I did not suffer from hunger because people gave me food. You only had to say you were out of work and someone would always help you out. But you can't carry on like that for ever. I began to realise that work had to be done in order to eat and sleep in a barracoon at least. By the time I decided to cut cane, I had already covered quite a bit of ground. I know all the part north of Las Villas well. It is the prettiest part of Cuba. That was where I started work.

The first plantation I worked on was called Purio. I turned up there one day in the rags I stood in and a hat

[63]

I had collected on the way. I went in and asked the over-seer if there was work for me. He said yes. I remember he was Spanish, with moustaches, and his name was Pepe. There were overseers in these parts until quite recently, the difference being that they didn't lay about them as they used to do under slavery. But they were men of the same breed, harsh, overbearing. There were still barra-coons after Abolition, the same as before. Many of them were newly built of masonry, the old ones having col-lapsed under the rain and storms. The barracoon at Purio was strong and looked as if it had been recently com-pleted. They told me to go and live there. I soon made myself at home, for it wasn't too bad. They had taken the bolts off the doors and the workers themselves had cut holes in the walls for ventilation. They no longer had to worry about escapes or anything like that, for the Negroes were free now, or so they said. But I could not help noticing that bad things still went on. There were bosses who still believed that the blacks were created for locks and bolts and whips, and treated them as before. It struck me that many Negroes did not know that things had changed, because they went on saying, 'Give me your blessing, my master.'

Those ones never left the plantation at all. I was dif-ferent in that I disliked having anything to do with the whites. They believed they were the lords of creation. At Purio I lived alone most of the time. I might have a concubine from Easter to San Juan's day; but women have always been selfish, and there wasn't a Christian soul alive who could support a black woman in those days.

Though I do say that women are the greatest thing there is. I was never short of a black woman to say, 'I want to live with you.'

I felt strange at first on the plantation. I went on feeling strange for about three months. I tired very easily, and my hands started to peel and my feet swelled up. I think it was the cane which did this, the cane together with the sun. Being so exhausted, I used to stay in the barracoon at night to rest. But in time I got used to it. I sometimes thought of going out at night, for there were dances and other amusements in the villages, but all I was after was a bit of fun with the chicks.

*

The work was exhausting. You spent hours in the fields and it seemed as if the work would never end. It went on and on until you were worn out. The overseers were always bothering you. Any worker who knocked off for long was taken off the job. I worked from six in the morning. The early hour did not bother me since in the forest it had been impossible to sleep late because of the cocks crowing. There was a break at eleven for lunch, which had to be eaten in the workers' canteen, usually standing because of the crowd of people squashed in. At one everyone went back to the fields. This was the worst and hottest time. Work ended at six in the afternoon. Then I would take myself off to the river, bathe for a while, and go back to get something to eat. I had to hurry because the kitchen did not work at night.

Food cost around six pesos a month. They gave good

[65]

portions, but it never varied: rice with black or white beans, or chick peas and jerked beef. Occasionally they slaughtered an old bullock. Beef is good meat, but I liked pork better and still do; it is more nourishing and strengthening. The best thing of all was the vegetables: sweet potato, malanga, yams. Corn meal too, but anyone who has to eat it day in day out soon gets tired of it. There was no shortage of meal. Some workers were in the habit of going to the overseer's office to get a chit authorising them to collect their food uncooked and take it to the barracoon. They then cooked it in their cooking-pots. The ones who had a regular woman would eat with her, as I did when I had a concubine. I no longer felt like putting up with the heat and crowding in the canteen.

The Negroes who worked at Purio had almost all been slaves; they were so used to life in the barracoon they did not even go out to eat. When lunch-time came they shut themselves up in their rooms to eat, and the same with dinner. They did not go out at night. They were afraid of people, and they said they would get lost if they did, they were convinced of this. I wasn't like that—if I got lost I always found myself again. When I think of the times I got lost in the forest and couldn't find a river!

On Sundays all the workers who wanted to could work overtime. This meant that instead of resting you went to the fields and cleared, cleaned or cut cane. Or if not that, you stayed in, cleaning out the troughs or scraping the boilers. This would only be in the morning. As there was nothing special to do that day, all the workers used to go and earn themselves extra money. Money is a very evil thing. A person who gets used to earning a lot is on the road to ruination. I earned the same as the rest. The pay worked out at around twenty-four pesos, including food. Some plantations paid twenty-five.

There were still plenty of taverns around to spend one's cash in. There were two or three at Purio. I used to go into them for a drink now and then, and I also went there if I wanted to buy something. To tell the truth, the taverns weren't very nice places. Almost every day fights would break out because of rivalries or jealousy over women. At night there were fiestas, and anyone who wanted could go. They were held in the mill compound. There was enough room to dance, and the Negroes them-selves sang the rumbas. The fun was in dancing and shout-ing and drinking. I never wholeheartedly took part in all that. I used to go and have a look when I felt like it; other-wise I stayed behind and rested. Time flew by. At nine sharp the rumba instruments had to be cleared away because the silence bell was ringing, the loudest bell they had, for people to go to bed. If the Negroes had had things their way, they would always have stayed dancing till dawn. I know how it is with them. Even now, if you go to a dance, the last person to leave will be a Negro. Person-ally, I won't say I don't like dancing and rumbas, but I have come to take a long view of these things. The next morning the workers got up feeling tired out, but they carried on as usual.

In those days you could get either permanent or tem-porary work on the plantations. Those employed on a permanent basis had to keep to a time-table. This way they would live in the barracoons and did not need to leave the plantations for anything. I preferred being a permanent worker myself, because the other life was too troublesome. A man who decided to free-lance would simply go along to a cane-field and, according to the amount of cane there, agree on a price. In those days fields of two or four *besanas** would work out at about thirty or forty pesos, and the work of clearing them would take fifteen or sixteen days. Those freelance workers were very sharp. They could rest whenever they felt like it, get a drink of water, and even took their women along to the cane-fields to lie with them. After the days had passed and the ground was thoroughly cleared, the overseer would come along and inspect it. If he found any botched work they had to go over it again. Then the overseer came back and, if he was satisfied, they would go off with their money to the towns to wait till the cane grew again. If their money ran out quickly, they would find some way of getting work on another plantation. They lived like tramps, bedding in the smaller rooms of the barracoons. They hardly ever took their women to their rooms, but used to see them at night because they were allowed out after the day's work.

With us fixed-rate workers things were different. We couldn't go out at night because at nine o'clock we had to be ready for the silence bell. I went out in the evenings on Sundays and I took my time. Some nights I got back after nine and nothing happened to me. They would

* A Spanish land measure equivalent to three square yards. Also a cane-field separated from others by furrows used as lanes for trucks and wagons.

open up and say, 'Get along, you're late back, you bastard!'

The barracoons were a bit damp, but all the same they were safer than the forest. There were no snakes, and all us workers slept in hammocks which were very comfortable, and one could wrap up well in the cold. Many of the barracoons were made of sacking. The one tiresome thing about them was the fleas; they didn't hurt, but you had to be up all night scaring them off with Spanish broom, which gets rid of fleas and ticks. All you had to do was sprinkle a little on the floor. Personally, I think all those insects came to Cuba as the Indians' revenge. The Indians laid a curse on Cuba. They are recovering their dead, Hatuey* and all his band.

At Purio, as on all plantations, there were Africans of various countries, but the Congolese were in the majority. It's not for nothing they call all the region in the north of Las Villas 'the Congo'. At that time there were Filipinos, Chinese, Canary Islanders, and an increasing number of Creoles there as well. They all worked on the cane, clearing the ground with spades and machetes and earthing up. Earthing up means ploughing with a bullock and a tree-trunk on a chain to turn over the soil, just as under slavery.

Relations between the groups remained unchanged. The Filipinos were as criminal as before. The Canary Islanders did not speak; the only thing that existed for them was work, and they were as arrogant as ever. They took against me because I wouldn't make friends with

* One of the most famous Indian chiefs of the time of the Conquistadores.

them. One had to be careful of the Islanders, because they knew a lot of magic and they would do anyone a bad turn. I think they earned more than the Negroes, although they always used to say that everyone earned the same amount. The overseer was the one who took care of the wages and kept all the accounts. He was an old Spaniard. Overseers were always old, because it takes a lot of experience to make up the accounts. He paid all the workers on the plantation. After the owner had reckoned up the profits, the overseer sent word for us to come and collect our pay. One by one, we would go into the office or storehouse, depending. Some people preferred to take all their pay in hard cash. Others, like me, preferred to have the overseer make out a chit for food to the store-keeper, so that they could go there and buy things on account. The store-keeper himself would hand over the money, half of it in food and drink and half in cash. Our way was better, because it meant you did not keep having to go along to the office to be looked up and down. I have always liked to be independent. Besides, the store-keepers were nice: Spaniards retired from the army.

In those days they paid you in Mexican or Spanish money. The Mexican money was silver, coins called *carandolesas*. There were also smaller coins worth twenty or forty cents and one peso. I remember one Spanish coin called Amadeo I. If you came across one of these, you didn't spend it but kept it as a good-luck token, because Amadeo I was King of Spain. It was pure silver like the Isabelina, which was worth fifty cents. Almost all the rest were gold. There were escudos worth two pesos, doubloons worth four pesos, centenes worth five pesos thirty cents, onzas and half-onzas.

These were the coins most used in Cuba till the coronation of Alfonso XIII. I learnt them off by heart so I couldn't be cheated. It was easier then because all of them had a king or queen's face on them, or a coat-of-arms. King Alfonso XIII began sending pesetas and silver pesos. The *calderilla* was copper money, and some coins were worth one cent and some two. Other coins came in too, like the *real fuerte*, which was worth fifteen cents. Twenty *reales fuertes*, if you reckon it up right, equal three pesos. This is true, no matter how you add it up. There are still people who use this old-fashioned method of counting. They seem to think humanity has made no progress. Although one may like old customs, it is silly to keep repeating them over and over like a record which has got stuck.

I felt better then than I do now. I had my youth. Now I still have my concubine from time to time, but it is not the same. A woman is a wonderful thing. Women, to tell the truth, are what I have got most pleasure from in my life. In the old days, when I was at Purio, I used to get up and go to the village on Sundays, always in the afternoons so as not to miss the morning's overtime, and sometimes I found myself a woman before even reaching the village. I was very bold; any pretty dark-skinned girl I met I got talking to, and they used to fall for me. I will say this, I always told them the truth: that I was a worker and liked sincerity. You couldn't play about with women like they do now. Not a chance! Women in those days were worth as much as men. They worked hard and they had no patience with feckless drifters. Once a woman trusted me I could even ask her for money. Now, she would consider very carefully whether I really needed it or not. If I did, she would give me all I asked for. If not, she would send me to fry asparagus. Those were the women in the old days.

When a man was short of women, he used to go to the fiesta on Sundays which were held in the villages nearest to the plantation. There were dances in the streets and in the clubs. The streets would be full of people dancing and enjoying themselves. I went only to find women, because I never liked dancing. They played cards and held horseback competitions. They put two poles far apart and tied a rope across and hung a ring from the rope, and the rider had to pass his stick, or *puá*, as they called it, through the ring. If he succeeded, he won the prize, which was usually to parade through town and be the proudest person there. Riders came from all the nearby villages for this event. I liked going to the places where the competitions were held to look at the horses, but I didn't like the way people used to quarrel and fight. The Negroes did not pay much attention to all this. They were spectators, for what Negro had a good horse?

The best entertainment was the cock-fights which were held on Sundays in all the villages. In Calabazar de Sagua, which was the one nearest to Purio, there was a very big cockpit. The pits were built of wood, painted red and white, the roofs made of planks with thick pieces of cardboard over the cracks. The fights were very bloody, but in those days every one went to them. Strange as it may seem, the blood was an attraction, it added to the sport and served to extract money from the small farmers who were just beginning to make their fortunes then. The workers used to bet too. Cock-fights were a vice and still are. Once you were inside a cockpit you just had to keep right on gambling, it was no place for misers or cowards. It was difficult not to lose your head while the fights were going on. The shouting was worse than the blood, and the heat was unbearable, but in spite of this all the men used to go along to try their luck, Negroes and whites alike. The problem was to find the money to bet with. Not many Negroes could. Aside from cock-fights and getting drunk, there was nothing else to do. It was better to take a woman into the forest and make love.

*

When San Juan's day, the 24th of June, came round, lots of villages held fiestas. It was a big day everywhere. There were celebrations at Calabazar, and I used to go along to watch. Everyone there wore their best clothes, men and women alike. The materials they used then were different from the ones now. Most of the men wore linen or striped shirts, fastened with gold buttons and very smart. They also wore clothes of fine drill, almud, which was a cloth as black as jet, and shiny alpaca, which was said to be the most expensive of the lot, though I never tried it. Thick frieze in a greyish colour was common too. It made the best trousers. I liked it because it didn't show the dirt.

[73]

In the old days men liked to dress well. I myself would never go to the village if I didn't have the clothes, and this despite the fact that we runaways had the reputation of being half wild—at least, that was the general opinion. If you compare the clothes they had then with the ones they use now, it is hard to see why in those days, in the warm weather, people didn't get unbearably hot.

Women's clothes were the last word. They looked like walking wardrobes. I think they hung just about everything they could find on themselves. They wore a chemise, petticoats, under-petticoats, stays, and, on top, a wide dress trimmed with coloured braid and bows. Almost all their clothes were of fine cambric. They also wore bustles. Bustles were little pillows the width of a buttock. They fastened these to their waists and let them hang down behind so their buttocks would tremble. Wearing a bustle was like having false flesh. Some of them used to pad their breasts. I don't know how they did it, but it looked real. Of course, I knew it was only cloth, but all the same, to see a woman like that, dressed up to the nines, was quite something. The ones without much hair wore hairpieces. The hairstyles were prettier than they are now and more natural. They did their own hair and they kept their hair long, because this was the Spanish fashion—fashion came from Spain, of course, never Africa. I didn't like women with short hair; they looked like boys. The fashion for short hair started when they opened hairdressers in Cuba. It wasn't even heard of before then. The women were the chief feature of the fiestas. They pretended that the reason why they dressed

themselves up was that they were so religious. Everything they wore was of good quality, and they liked you
to know it. Gold ear-rings and bracelets, shoes of all sorts,
like high-heeled calf boots with a little metal tip on them,
to protect the toe. The shoes were buttoned. There was
one sort of boot called 'Polish', which buttoned up the
side. The men wore elastic-sided boots—the rich ones,
that is. I, for instance, only had one pair of low-cut
leather shoes and my cowhide ones.

The fiestas of San Juan were the most celebrated ones
in the region. Two or three days before the 24th the
village children would start getting ready for it, decora-
ting the houses and the church with palm-leaves. The
grown-ups organised dances in clubs. Even then there
were Negro clubs, with a saloon and a room for dancing.
The entrance fee went towards club funds. I sometimes
took off my straw hat and went in, but I left again almost
at once because of the crush of people. Outdoor workers
found it hard to get used to dancing in a closed-in place.
Besides, the time to catch the girls was when they left.
When I saw a woman leaving, I used to go up and ask her
to have a drink or something to eat. There were always
stalls where they sold sandwiches, sausages, *tamales*,
cider and beer. Now they call them kiosks. The beer was
T-brand, Spanish. It cost twenty-five centavos and was
ten times stronger than the modern stuff. People who knew
about beer liked it for its bitter flavour. I used to knock
back a few, and afterwards I felt in high spirits.

The cider was good too, and much drunk, especially
at christenings. They say that cider is gold water, sacred.

Rioja wine was very popular. I knew about it from slavery. It cost twenty-five *reales* for a large carafe. You could get a glass for one *real* or a half-*real*, depending on the size. That wine made all the women tipsy. I tell you, it was quite something to see one of those females lurching drunkenly off into the forest.

Although it was a religious festival and there were altars even in the doorways of the houses, I never got around to praying. I didn't see many other men praying either. They went there to drink and pick up women. The streets were full of vendors selling popcorn, biscuits and cakes, grapefruit, coconuts and soft drinks.

It was the custom at fiestas to dance the *caringa*, which was one of the white man's dances. It was performed by couples holding handkerchiefs, and whole groups used to dance it in the parks and in the streets. It was amusing to watch because the people used to leap about a lot to the sound of accordions, gourds and kettle-drums. And they sang:

> *Toma y toma y toma caringa!*
> *Pa la vieja palo y jeringa.**

They danced the *zapateo* as well, the traditional Cuban dance, and the *tumbandera*. The *zapateo* was very graceful and not so indecent as the African dances—the dancers' bodies hardly touched each other. It was performed in people's homes or in the countryside, and it did not have

---

* The full version goes:
  Dance, dance, dance the *caringa*!
  For the old woman the stick and syringe.
  Dance, dance, dance the *caringa*!
  For the old man the stick and clay pipe.
Any sexual symbolism is not accidental.

to be on any special day, the 24th of June would do as well as St James's day. To dance it the women wore sprays of flowers in their hair, cultivated flowers, not wild ones, fine cambric dresses embroidered with ribbons, and red and white kerchiefs. The men wore kerchiefs too, and straw hats. The women stood facing the men, holding their skirts up in both hands and tapping their heels, while the men watched and laughed and circled round them with their hands behind their backs. Sometimes a a woman would pick a man's hat off the ground and put it on for a joke, but when the other men saw her doing this they all threw their hats down and their partners picked them up and put them on. The women dancers were given presents of money or flowers. Flowers were very popular then, there were flowers everywhere. You never see flowers now like there were on fiesta days. They were used to decorate all the houses; people tied blossoms to a wire and made garlands along their balconies. The families themselves would throw flowers into the street at all the passers-by. They had this rose, a great big one, called the Bourbon rose. That and the lily were the ones they sold most of. The lily is white and strongly perfumed.

They sold the best flowers in the Spanish colony, roses and carnations, and it was there they danced the *jota*. The *jota* was exclusively for the Spanish. They brought this dance to Cuba and would not let anyone else dance it. I used to stop in the doorways of the Spanish colony and look in to watch them. The *jota* was pretty to watch because of the costumes and the noise of the castanets. They threw up their arms and laughed like

[77]

idiots. The whole night went by like that. Sometimes the Spanish themselves would notice how people were crowding round the windows to watch, and then they came out and handed round wine, grapes and cheese. I drank a lot of Spanish wine by dint of standing in doorways.

The *tumbandera* was another popular dance. This has vanished as well. The whites didn't dance it because they said it was a vulgar Negro dance. I didn't like it myself, I must admit. The *jota* was more elegant. The *tumbandera* was more like the rumba, very lively and always danced by a man and a woman. They played two little drums like the *tumbadoras*, but much smaller, and maraccas. It was sometimes danced in the streets and also in the Negro clubs.

The fiestas now are not as gay as they used to be. They are more modern or something. The fact is, one really enjoyed oneself in those days. Even I, who only went along to watch, used to have a good time. The people used to dress up in different sorts of costumes in brilliant colours and put on cardboard and cloth masks to look like devils, monkeys or pierrots. If a man wanted to be revenged on another for some reason, he would dress up as a woman and lash out at his enemy with his whip when he saw him go by. Then he ran away. That way no one could track him down.

They organised various games for the San Juan fiestas. The one I remember best was played with a duck. The game was a little cruel because you had to kill the duck first. When it was dead it was taken by the legs and stuffed with grease so that it shone, then hung from a rope slung between two poles across the street. More people went to see this game than the dancing. When the duck was in place the riders came out. Starting at a distance of ten metres, they came at a gallop (they had to get up speed, otherwise it didn't count), and when they got level with the duck they tugged at its head with all their might. The rider who pulled it off was given a scarlet sash and made President of the Ball. As President he received other favours; all the women crowded round him at once. If he was engaged they put another sash around his fiancée and named her Lady President. That night they both presided together over the ball, they were the first couple to take the floor, and people threw flowers at them.

In the morning, round ten o'clock, the *juá** was set alight. The *juá* was a wooden figure shaped like a man, strung up on a rope in the middle of the street, representing the Devil. The boys set fire to it, and as it was covered with paper it caught at once. You could see all the coloured papers burning in the air, and the head and arms. I watched this many years running because the custom lingered on. On San Juan's day everyone went down to the river to bathe, because if you didn't you would soon be crawling with bugs. If there was anyone who couldn't go down to the river, an old man or a very young child, they got into a tub, which wasn't the same thing, but at least it held water, which was the important part. The more you poured over yourself the cleaner you came out. I had a black mistress who hated water like a cat, but even so she used to immerse herself in the river fully dressed on San Juan's day.

* A contraction of Judas.

*

As the *santeros** held their own festival that day as
well, I would leave a little spare time to go along and see
them at night. I visited various houses of worship, greeted
the people there and the saints, and then went home to
sleep. It was the custom on that day for godchildren to
bring money to their godparents, and anything else they
asked for. To a Negro godparents are most important
people, because they give him a saint. The fiestas in the
Casas de Santo were good ones. Only Negroes went to
them, the Spanish didn't approve of *santería*. But with
time this changed, and now you can see white high priests
with red cheeks. *Santería* used to be a religion for
Africans, and even the Civil Guards, the pure-blooded
ones, would have nothing to do with it. They would
make some remark in passing like, 'What's going on here?',
and the Negroes would say, 'We're celebrating San Juan.'
But of course it was not San Juan but Oggún, the god of
war—*Oggún Arere, Oggún Oke, Oggún Aguanillé*†—the
most famous god in the whole region then. He is always
found in the countryside and they dress him in green or
purple.

You had to behave very respectably at those festivals,
and if you didn't really believe, you had to keep this quiet.
Negroes don't like interlopers, they never have. So I
always went along very quietly, listened to the drumming,
watched the Negroes and afterwards had something to
eat. There was always lots of different food. My favourite

* Priests of *santería*, or saint worship, a matriarchal religion of
Yoruba origin but overlaid with Catholic elements. It is still strong in
Cuba today, and followers include many whites as well as Negroes.

† The Yoruba god Oggún in his three aspects—warrior, hunter and
metal-worker.

dish was *harina de amalá*, which was the food of the god Changó. It was made of corn meal and water; the corn was boiled to remove the husk, and then thrown into a mortar and ground down to a paste. This *amalá*, as it was called, was wrapped in banana leaves into the shape of balls and could be eaten with or without sugar.

Then there was *calalú*, which is eaten like okra. It was made with wild amaranth and spices of all sorts, and when well seasoned it was delicious. It tasted best eaten with your hands. Another dish they had was *guengeré*, made with beef, rice and the little *guengeré* leaf. There are two sorts of *guengeré* leaf, the white and the mauve. The white was nicer, smoother to taste.

They ate *masango*, too, maize gently simmered. I believe this was also a Congolese dish. *Cheketé* was the *santeros'* favourite drink, and they always provided it at their feasts. It was something like a cold chocolate drink but made with orange juice and vinegar. Children drank it a lot. It tasted a bit like *atol*, the drink made with yucca or sago; the yucca was ground to the consistency of starch. It was meant to be taken by the spoonful, but greedy people filled up their glasses to the top. But the most delicious of all these dishes was *ochinchín*, made from watercress, greens, almonds and stewed prawns. *Ochinchín* was Ochún's* food.

All the saints had their special foods. Obatalá had a dish of kidney beans, and there were many others I can't remember. A lot of these dishes were harmful to eat; pumpkin, for instance, which must not be eaten because

* The Yoruba god of gold and sexuality.

many of the saints won't touch it. Even now people don't eat pumpkin. I never looked for it even when I was in the forest, because it is dangerous to get tangled up in a pumpkin plant, you break out in a rash all over and you can't stand on your legs for long.

I never ate sesame seed either, because it brought me out in spots and swellings. If the saints try to stop you eating something they must have a good reason, and I don't take that sort of risk, even for fun. Even now I don't touch these things, whatever the priest may say.

One should respect religions even if one is not a great believer. In those days even the most uncivilised people believed. The Spaniards were all believers. The proof of this is that all work stopped at Purio plantation on the feasts of St James and Santa Ana, and the place fell silent. The sugar-boiling stopped and the fields were deserted. It was like a shrine there. The priests came in the morning and started praying and kept it up for hours. I hardly understood a word and didn't pay much attention to it. To be honest, I have never cared for priests. Some of them were the next thing to criminals. They flirted with pretty white women and slept with them, they were lecherous and pious both at once. If they had a child they would pass it off as a godson or nephew; they hid them under their cassocks and never said, 'This is my son.'

They kept tabs on the Negroes, though, and if a black woman gave birth she had to send for the priest within three days or she would be in hot water with the plantation-owner. That was how all the children came to be Christians.

[82]

If a priest went by, you were supposed to say, 'A blessing, Father.' Sometimes they didn't so much as look at you. Many Spaniards and Canary Islanders are like that, though not the Galicians.

Priests and lawyers were sacred in those days, because their titles won them great respect. Even someone who had passed his baccalaureate was thought very grand. But Negroes were never any of these things, least of all priests. I never saw a black priest. The priesthood was for whites of Spanish descent. You had to be Spanish before you could even become a watchman, although a watchman does nothing but keep an eye on things. They earned six pesos a month.

At Purio there was a fat one who was a Spaniard. He rang the work bell and the silence bell, that was all he did. It must have been the easiest life ever. I would have liked to be a watchman, that was my ambition, but I never left the fields at Purio. I had arms like masts as a result. In spite of everything the sun in the cane-fields is good for you. It must be the reason I have lived so long.

*

But life grew wearisome on the plantations. It was boring to see the same people and fields day after day. The hardest thing was to get used to one place for a long time. I had to leave Purio because life seemed to have stopped still there. I started walking south, and I got to San Agustin Ariosa sugar-mill, near the village of Zulueta. At first I did not intend to stop there because I preferred walking and I was going on to Remedios, but as luck would have it I found myself a mistress there and so I stayed. I liked that woman. She was pretty and blueish-black, one of those cheeky mulatto women who don't care a fig for anyone. Her name was Ana. But I grew bored with her as time went on. That Ana put the wind up me with her witchcraft. Every night it was the same story, spirits and witches. At last I said to her, 'I've had enough of you, witch.' She went on her way and I never saw her again. Then I found another mistress, a black-skinned Negress, black as the soil. This one wasn't a witch, but she had a very exuberant nature. I left her after two or three years. She was too jolly for me. But she wasn't the only happy one. As soon as you turned up at the plantation for work, the women would gather round and there was always one who wanted to live with you.

I stayed a long time at Ariosa. When I arrived the other workers asked me, 'Hey, where are you from?' I said, 'I am a freed slave from Purio.' Then they took me to the overseer who gave me work. He put me on to cane-cutting. It didn't seem strange to me; I was an expert at it by then. I also hoed the cane-fields.

The plantation was of medium size, owned by a man called Ariosa, a pure-blooded Spaniard. It was one of the first plantations to become a mill, and a large-gauge line ran through it, bringing the cane direct from the fields to the boiler-house. It was much the same there as any-where else. There were the usual yes-men and toadies to masters and overseers alike. They always questioned new workers to discover their views. This was on account of the hatred which has always existed between the groups

of slaves, because of ignorance. This is the only reason
for it. The freed slaves were generally very ignorant and
would lend themselves to anything. It even happened
that if some fellow became a nuisance, his own brothers
would undertake to kill him for a few centenes.

The priests interfered in everything. If they said a
Negro was troublesome, he had to watch out, otherwise
he would find someone ready to dispose of him at the
first available opportunity.

Religion was strong at Ariosa. There was a church
nearby, but I never went because I knew the priests were
the real supporters of the inquisition in Cuba; I say this
because the priests were known to do certain things.
They were devils with women. They turned the sacristy
into a brothel. Anyone who has lived in Ariosa knows the
stories, they even got to the barracoons. I know quite a
few, and some things I saw myself.

The priests put women in dungeons, in holes where
they had torturers ready to murder them. Other dungeons were full of water and the poor wretches drowned.
This has been told me many times.

I saw priests with loose women who slept with them
and afterwards said, 'Father, a blessing.' They also talked
at Ariosa of what life was like in the churches and
monasteries. The priests were like other men, but they
had all the gold, and they didn't spend it. I never saw a
priest enjoying himself in a tavern. They shut themselves
up in their churches and there they wasted away. They
made collections every year for the church, for the saints'
vestments and flowers.

I don't believe the question of the sugar-mills ever interested them. They never went as far as the machines. They were afraid of suffocating or being deafened. They were the most delicate people imaginable.

In those days the machines were driven by steam. I once went into the mill, and as I went near the grinder it began to cough. I had to leave at once, because my body wasn't accustomed to such heat. The fields are different with their vegetation and the dampness which clings to your skin.

The best work I did at Ariosa was in the mill, or near it, because it meant I could leave the fields. I really enjoyed that job. I had to spread out the cane on the conveyor-belt. This was done inside, where there was still a breeze blowing. The belt was as long as a palm-tree. They brought the carts full of cane and backed it up to the belt, then four or six of us unloaded the cane and spread it out, after which the belt started to run along its rollers until it reached the grinder. It deposited the cane in the grinder and then went back for more. You couldn't waste time over this job because the overseers were there keeping watch.

It was easy work, though, and working with the mixer was easy too, and more enjoyable. Here the job was to fill up little carts. These went empty to the boilers, were filled up there with fresh sugar and then sent to the mixer. When the boilers emptied they had to be washed down with powerful hoses. The mixer was a big machine with hooks and a gutter into which the sugar was deposited. The mixer ground the sugar, which then went to the centrifuge to be refined, without your having to lift a finger. The boilers used to froth over every twenty-four hours, then the whistle blew loud enough to deafen you. That meant you had to be ready to collect the *templa*, which was what we called the stuff spewed up.

These were the jobs I did at Ariosa. I never fell asleep. Anyone who slept was punished, and if the overseer got really angry he threw him out into the street. At night I went into the barracoon and fell asleep at once. I don't know which is more tiring, the forest or the mills.

I used to dream a good bit in those days, but I never dreamed visions. A dream comes through the imagination. If you think hard about a certain plantain tree and look at it, tomorrow or the day after you will dream about it. I dreamt about work and women. Work is a bad thing to dream about. It frightens you, and then the next day you think you are still dreaming, and that is when you can catch your finger in a machine or slip.

Women are good for dreams. I was once in love with a Moorish Negress who haunted my dreams. I had a strange old time of it with that woman. She took no notice of me. I still remember her from time to time. And I remember Mama. Mama was an old Negress who used to go into the men's rooms, say, 'How are you all?' and have a good look round before going to the overseer and telling him what she had seen. Bitch and spy! Everyone was afraid of her wagging tongue. She had several mulatto children, but she never talked about their father. My guess is that it was the overseer. They always gave her light work to do. She served meals and washed clothes: shirts, trousers, and the linen children's trousers (called *mamelucos*) with straps over the shoulders. Little boys in those days wore nothing else. They were brought up wild and uneducated. The only thing they were taught was raising vegetables and hoeing; but no learning. They were often beaten, and if they went on being naughty they were made to kneel on grains of rice or corn. A whipping was the most common punishment. The parents came and then the boy was beaten with a birch or piece of braided rope until the blood ran. The cane was a green switch which never broke even when it was wielded violently enough to flay the skin. I believe I had sons, maybe many or maybe not, but I don't think I would ever have punished them like that.

In the taverns they sold red whip-lashes made of twisted rawhide. Mothers kept them fastened to their belts, and if a child misbehaved they hit out at him. These savage punishments were a hangover from slavery. The children today are naughtier. They were quiet enough in the old days and really did not deserve such punishment. Now they are spanked instead of being whipped, and this has changed them. A child in those days spent the day running about the yard or playing with marbles which came in all colours and were sold in the taverns. Seven or ten boys would play, in two teams. They drew two lines on the ground and threw marbles in turn, and the one who came nearest the lines won. Then they all threw again, and a player who touched one of the other team's marbles scored.

They also played *tejo*, and the girls amused themselves

making rag dolls or playing the ring game with the boys. The boys dropped the ring into the hand of the girl they liked best. They spent hours at it, especially in the evenings, from six until they went to bed at eight or nine. They still rang the silence bell at Ariosa at the same time as before, nine sharp.

Children were always playing truant. They would come scavenging round the houses to get out of work, and they often used to hide to escape from punishments their parents threatened them with. The children no longer received Christian instruction, but some of their parents were bitten by the Christianity craze and used to take them off to church. The church was very important to the Spaniards, and they taught the Negroes about it every single day. But neither Lucas nor I ever went. Both the Fabas were magic-men. One was called Lucas, and the other Ricardo or Regino. I was friends with Lucas. They had been slaves on the Santa Susana plantation, which was somewhere between Lajas and Santo Domingo and belonged to Count More. Lucas talked a lot about him. He said he was one of the cruellest Spaniards he had ever come across, fearing no one. He gave orders and you had to obey. Even the Governors were in awe of him. Governor Salamanca once ordered him to be arrested because he was paying his Negroes with gambling chips stamped with the T of the Holy Trinity. The Count collected money in gold and silver coin and paid out in paper notes. He was an armed robber. The King of Spain got to hear of this and ordered the Governor to make a thorough investigation. Salamanca went out to the plantation in disguise, and when he arrived he sat down in the tavern and ordered a meal. No one knew he was the Governor. He took notes on everything he saw in a little book. And when he was well informed of the dreadful things the Count was doing, he sent for him and said, 'Come to Government House.' But the Count replied, 'It is no further from your house to mine. You come here.' Salamanca refused. He sent the Civil Guard instead, and they brought the Count to Havana in handcuffs and imprisoned him, and he died within a few months. Then the other counts and viscounts looked for a way of revenging themselves on the Governor. They made friends with Salamanca's doctor, and persuaded him to poison the Governor. This was done some time in the year '90 by way of a growth on his leg. Instead of curing it the doctor poisoned him through it and the Governor died a few days later. Lucas told me all about this because he saw it—it happened the year he came to Ariosa with Regino.

Lucas was a great magic-man, and fond of the *maní* dance. He was a good dancer. He was always saying to me, 'Why don't you learn to dance *maní*?' And I said, 'No, because if someone punched me I'd lay him out.' Lucas knew a lot of things. He danced *maní* so as to get a swarm of women round him. When a man was a good *maní* dancer the women would say, 'Hell, I go for that man!' and then they would take him to the cane-fields to make love, because cane straw keeps you warm and smells good in cold weather. This thing of going to the cane-fields to screw was a common practice, the people made use of the wagon track between the mill and the cane-fields. In those days you grabbed any woman and took her into the cane. There wasn't all the courtship there is now. If a woman went with a man she knew she would have to get down on her back.

Lucas was a good fellow, but overfond of women. Sometimes he and I would get a gang together to play *monte* in the barracoon at night. We put a tarpaulin down on the ground and sat down to play all night. When I found I had won four to six pesos I used to leave. And if I was losing too much, I beat it quick. I wasn't the sort of guy who sits around losing all night just out of bravado. Besides, the games always ended badly. There were fights and rows. Men are very selfish. They always have been. If one man didn't think he should have lost, there was one hell of a row. As I've always kept out of that sort of thing, I would leave.

There were two Negroes at Ariosa who had known me when I was a boy. One day they told Lucas, 'He led a dog's life in the forest.' I saw them later and I said, 'Listen, you were the ones who lived like dogs, because you used to get whipped.' The truth is, all those folk who didn't run away believed that we runaways were animals. The world is full of fools. You have to go through something before you can know what it is like. I don't know what a mill looks like inside unless I look. That's what happened to them. Lucas agreed with me, because he knew me well. He was my one real friend.

They didn't give work to just anyone at Ariosa. If someone turned up dressed very smartly, with a natty little straw hat, they wouldn't look at him because they said he must be a pimp. If you wanted to get work it was better to go along to the plantations looking a bit shabby, in a hat made of palm-leaves. The overseers said the dandies weren't up to a good job of work, and at Ariosa you had to work hard. They watched you the whole time, and they would book you for nothing at all. I remember a criminal by the name of Camilo Polavieja, who was Governor of Cuba in the Nineties. No one liked him. He said the workers were cattle and he had kept the same views as he had during slavery. Once he ordered all the workers without cards to be given the *componte*. The cards were slips of paper—like chits—with the worker's address on. Anyone caught without his card got a good belting across the shoulders with a dried bull's pizzle, that was the *componte*. It was always given in gaol, because that's where they took you if you were caught without your card. The card cost twenty-five cents; you got it from the town hall, and it had to be renewed every year.

Polavieja did other horrible things besides the *componte*. He smashed Negroes' heads in by the thousand. He was as arrogant as a bull, even with his own troops; the soldiers themselves said so. Once he hit on the idea of sending Negroes to the island of Fernando Poo, a terrible punishment because it was a desert island, a place of crocodiles and sharks. They let the Negroes loose there, and there was no way they could escape. Thieves, pimps, cattle-rustlers and rebels were all sent there, and anyone with a tattoo mark, because tattoos were said to be a sign of rebellion against the Spanish

Government. The *Náñigos** were sent away as well to the islands of Ceuta and Chafarinas, because Polavieja said they were anarchists. Workers who weren't involved either in *nañiguismo* or the revolution stayed in Cuba. Women weren't sent away either; those islands were for men only.

Polavieja also made the women carry identification papers, which were issued to them in the town hall. The women had a lot of medical attention in those days. A doctor used to go to Ariosa every Monday to examine them, a Spanish doctor, but quite unknown, a nobody. No one had any faith in the Spanish doctors. It was still witchcraft which cured people. Witch-doctors and Chinese doctors were the most highly thought of. There was one Chinese doctor from Canton called Chin, who used to go round the countryside curing rich people. I saw him once in the village of Jicotea, and I haven't forgotten him. The Madrazos, who were a rich family, had sent for him. Chin was short and plump, and he wore a shabby-looking doctor's tunic and a straw hat. The poor people only knew him at a distance because he charged a lot for his services. It wouldn't surprise me if he cured people with the same herbs they put in bottles and sell in the pharmacies today.

There were lots of Chinese in Cuba, they came there as indentured workers. As time went by they grew old and left the fields. I used to go out of the plantation quite a bit and I saw a lot of them, especially in Sagua la

---

* Members of a secret society of southern Nigerian origin, which sets great store by virility and excludes women. It still exists in Cuba.

Grande, which was their neighbourhood. Plenty of workers went to Sagua on Sundays, from all the plantations round about. That's how I came to see the Chinese theatre. The theatre was large, made of wood, very well built. The Chinese had a lot of talent for this sort of thing. They painted everything in bright colours and on the stage they made grimaces and climbed on to each other's shoulders. The people applauded wildly, and the Chinese bowed politely. The Chinese were the most elegant thing in Cuba. Everything they did was in silence, bowing away the whole time. They were well trained.

They had their own clubs in Sagua la Grande where they met and talked their own languages and read the Chinese newspapers aloud. They probably only did it to be annoying, but as no one understood a word of what they were saying they went on reading as cool as anything.

The Chinese were very clever at business. They had their own shops which sold all sorts of peculiar things, paper dolls for children, perfumes and materials. The whole of Tacon Street in Sagua was owned by Chinese. They also had tailor's shops, sweet-shops and opium dens there. The Chinese were very fond of opium, I don't think they knew it was harmful. They smoked it in long wooden pipes, hidden away at the back of their shops so the whites and Negroes shouldn't see them, although no one was ever persecuted for smoking opium in those days.

Another thing they enjoyed was gambling. They always were and still are the world's greatest inventors of

gambling games, and they played them in the streets and
doorways. I remember one game they called 'the button'
and another one which has survived till today, called
'charades'. Both whites and Negroes went to Sagua to
play with them, but the only game I used to play was
monte.

The Chinese rented a house to meet in on fiesta days
and gambled there till they dropped. They used to have a
doorman to attend to the players and also to stop rows
from breaking out. The doorman wouldn't let the local
toughs go in.

I went to Sagua whenever I could, either by train or on
foot, more often walking, because the train was expensive.
I knew the Chinese held festivals on their important
religious days. The village would be packed with people
who had come to watch them celebrate. They did all
sorts of acrobatics and mime shows. I was never able to
go to any of these fiestas of theirs, but I heard that they
used to hang by their pigtails and their bodies would
dance about high in the air. Another trick they did was
for one of them to lie on the ground with a millstone on
his belly, and another would pick up a great big hammer
and give the stone a colossal crack without hurting him
at all. Then the first Chinese jumped to his feet and
laughed and the audience shouted, 'More, more!' Or
they used to burn papers like the puppeteers at Remedios
and fling them on the ground till they were burnt to
ashes, then rake the ashes and pull out coloured streamers.
This is perfectly true, because I was told about it many
different times. Those Chinese hypnotised their audi-

ences. This is something they have always known how to do. It is the foundation of their religion.

Later they went over to selling vegetables and fruit and began losing money. The Chinese have lost the cheerfulness they had in Spanish times. If you see a Chinese now and ask him, 'How are you?' he says, 'Me not know.'

*

Although I stayed several years at Ariosa I am beginning to forget things about it now. Time is the best help for the memory. If you try to remember something which happened recently you can't, but the further back you go the more clearly you see it all. There were lots of workers at Ariosa, I think it must have been one of the biggest plantations of the time. Everyone spoke well of it. The owner was an innovator and made many changes in the mills. Some plantations gave very bad food because the cooks didn't care, but Ariosa wasn't like that, you ate well there. If the cooks got careless, the owner used to come and tell them to take more trouble. Some plantations were still the way they had been under slavery; the owners still thought they owned the blacks. This was true of the plantations furthest away from the towns.

When the dead season came everything stopped. Things were quite different from usual in the plantation and the sugar-mill town. But no one stayed completely idle —the slack season went on a long time, and if you didn't work you didn't eat. You had to keep doing something.

I spent a lot of time looking for women during those

months, walking through the villages. But I always went back to the barracoon at night. I could get to Sagua la Grande, Zulueta and Rodrigo by train, but I didn't fancy knowing too many people in those villages. When you come down to it, the plantation was my life. My job during the slack season was usually hoeing the cane-fields, that was the thing I knew best. Occasionally I was given the edges to do, still hoeing but along the verges so all the cane wouldn't burn up if there was a fire. They planted new cane too, and I had to turn the earth over thoroughly to make it grow well. The cane-fields were ploughed with just one bullock and a small plough. The bullock went along the cane furrow with a teamster guiding the plough and the *narigonero*,* a boy of eight or nine, leading the animal so he wouldn't go crooked.

There was less work and fewer duties at this time, and this naturally led to boredom. I used to go to the villages whenever I had the cash, but if I didn't, what the hell could I hope to do with myself? Then it was better to stay in the barracoon.

The women carried on as usual, there was no such thing as a dead time for them. They washed the men's clothes, mended and sewed. Women worked harder in those days than they do now.

They had plenty of other things to do, like raising pigs and chickens. There were allotments still, but not many. I think the Negroes lost interest in them after Abolition. But those who still had one worked on it during the slack time. I never had an allotment myself, because I didn't

* Literally 'holder of the nose-ring'.

have a family. Another thing many people did was raise fighting-cocks. The plantation-owners were mad about fighting-cocks from way back, it was really a vice with them. They loved those cocks more than they did people.

Some workers, both blacks and whites, spent the dead time looking after the boss's fighting-cocks. The small farmers had their little cocks too, but they weren't up to much, not like the expensive thoroughbreds. The cock-breeders won a lot of money betting, staking a cock's spur at eight to ten gold ounces. If a cock was wounded in the fight its trainer had to treat it at once, and this needed a lot of experience because those cocks were very delicate. Sometimes a cock would be hurt so badly that they picked it up half-dead. The trainer would blow down its beak to get the blood-clots out and revive it, then they threw it back into the ring, and as long as it went on fighting it had not lost. A cock either had to drop dead or run away for the fight to be over. That was the only end possible.

I went to a lot of cock-fights in the pits near Ariosa. I liked to see them, although I have always thought it a cruel sport. I remember I took a clay pipe with me, which I bought in a local store for half a dollar or thereabouts. I filled it with a plug of tobacco and puffed away at it to while away the time. If anyone got bored at those fights it was because they wanted all the hurly-burly and excitement of fiestas and carnivals.

*

In the old days any slave who died was buried in the

cemetery on the plantation, but then people began to hear groans and see white lights moving to and fro above the graves. The accumulation of dead in the plantations at that time led to a lot of witchcraft. That was why they took them to the big cemetery in the village after Abolition. Four of the dead man's friends would carry him there in a coffin on two stout planks of hard wood or wild cane, each plank shouldered by two men so as to distribute the weight evenly. The coffin, made by a carpenter on the plantation, was of cheap soft wood, pine while the candle-holders were made of hollowed-out banana stumps. There were four candles, like today. The dead would be laid out where they had lived, in their shacks or in the barracoon.

In those days it was not the custom to take them to a funeral parlour. There were cases of corpses coming back to life because they had been buried too quickly, and so the custom of waiting twenty-four hours before burial arose. This is the modern way, but even this does not seem to be foolproof because I have heard of corpses struggling up, thin and ill, after being buried, and screaming and screaming.

Many of those cases occurred during a cholera epidemic. Anyone who looked a bit moribund was taken away in the cart and buried. Later they walked away as if nothing had happened. The people were terrified.

When a worker died the plantation was crowded with people. Everyone came to pay their respects. There was comradeship and reverence. A death was a very big thing in those days. The dead person's whole family came riding in from other plantations or faraway villages. Work went on, but people looked depressed. I couldn't keep still after I heard someone had died because I was afraid the spirit would walk.

They dressed the dead up in their best clothes, even their rawhide shoes, and buried them like that. There was always a great deal of food that day. In the evening they served vegetables, rice and pork, white wine and T-brand beer. At night there was white Creole and yellow Spanish cheese and coffee the whole time, coffee the way I like it, served in hollow gourds grown specially for this. That's the only way to drink coffee.

If the dead man had relatives they would see to all these preparations, otherwise the man's friends and their wives would club together and do it all between them. When the dead man's family was posh, they served coffee in big white china cups. After everyone had talked and eaten, the body was taken without more ado to be buried in the main cemetery. And if you want my opinion, it's best not to die, because a few days later no one remembers you, not even your closest friends. It's silly to make such a fuss of the dead, like people do nowadays, because it's nothing but hypocrisy really. It always has been. For my part, I want my fiestas while I'm alive.

*

One of the funny things about those days was courting. When a young man had his eye on a girl he would use thousands of tricks. They didn't set about these things the way they do now, quite openly. There was

more mystery; and tricks, all sorts of tricks. If I wanted
to make a respectable woman fall for me, I dressed myself
in white and walked right by her without looking at her.
I did this several days running until the time came when
I decided to ask her something. The women liked seeing
men dressed in white. A black man like me in white was
something which caught the eye. A hat was an essential
piece of equipment, because you could do a thousand and
one things with it: put it on, take it off, raise it to a
woman and ask, 'Well, how are you, then?'

If a courting couple, but particularly the girl, had
parents, they courted each other with little stones and
grains of corn. The girl would stand at the front door
and as the man went by he would say, 'Psss-pss,' or
whistle, and when she looked round he would smile and
start throwing the little stones one by one. She responded
by picking them up and keeping them. If she didn't keep
them it meant she didn't fancy him. Haughty, conceited
women would probably throw the stones right back.

The couple would meet later at some evening entertainment, at a wake or one of the fiestas or carnivals. If the
girl had accepted his advances she would say, 'Listen, I've
still got that corn you threw at me, here it is.' Then he
would hold her hand or kiss her. She would ask, 'Are you
coming round to my house?' He would say yes, and the
next day he would be round there to speak to her parents.
The girl would pretend, because women always do, that
she didn't know anything about this, and she might even
say, 'I have to think it over.' The house would be made
ready days before the wedding and the girl's mother

helped in all the to-do. The couple would already own a dozen stools, a big bed, a Saratoga trunk and all the cooking things they needed. The poor didn't know about cupboards in those days. The rich had them, but without glass windows, tall cupboards like horses of cedarwood.

The custom was for the girl's parents and the couple's godparents to give the groom half a dozen chickens, a large sow, a young heifer, a milch cow and the wedding dress, which had to have a train because she was not allowed to show her ankles. Any woman who did was not religious or respectable. The man provided for the home; he was the head of the household. She carried out his orders and to begin with did no outside work except perhaps a little washing for some family or other. Once they were settled in their routine they began receiving visitors, and they would talk about the wedding reception and the beer and food they had served there. Every morning the girl's mother or her old man would come round and pay a duty-call.

The priest might call round too, although they were more concerned about visiting the rich people. All those saintly types were after was cash. When people were married they had to pay six or seven pesos, rich and poor alike. Poor people, plantation workers, were married in the chapel, which was at the back of the church. Rich people were married right in the middle, in front of the main altar, and they had benches with cushions on them, whereas the poor sat on wooden stools in the chapel or sacristy, as it was sometimes called.

As a rule the guests didn't go into the chapel but waited outside for the couple to come out. When a man married a widow they used to blow the *fotuto* and bang tin cans in his face to tease him. They did this because the 'widower', as they called him, was like a brick-layer— filling up a hole made by someone else. The angrier the man got the more they blew the *fotuto* and banged their cans. But if he said, 'All right, lads, let's all go and drink,' they shut up and accepted the invitation. That was the way men of experience behaved. But if one of those in-experienced, overgrown boys fell in love with a widow, he always got furious and behaved like an animal. That was the way to make your friends hate you.

A good character matters in everything. If you live alone, it isn't necessary, but since we live surrounded by people it's better to make oneself pleasant, not fall out with them. Those widows were shameless. There was one at Ariosa who married one of the men there. When they blew the *fotuto* at him after the wedding, she looked embarrassed and hid her face, but she was only pre-tending. One day she went into the bushes with another man and they caught her at it. When she came back no one would speak to her.

Casual relationships were more convenient. The women were free and they didn't have to get along with their parents. They worked in the fields, helping in the hoeing and sowing, and they went with a man when they felt like it. The easy-going fellows always went in for this kind of arrangement, one woman one day, another the next. I think this is the better way myself. I stayed free and didn't marry till I was old; I was a bachelor in many places. I knew women of all colours, proud women and kind ones.

I had an old Negress in Santa Clara after the war. She had all these crazy ideas about me. She even asked me to marry her. I told her straight out, no. But we lived together and she told me, 'I want you to inherit my house.' She owned a big house with lots of rooms in the Condado district, San Cristobal Street. A few days before her death she called me and said I was to inherit everything. She wrote me a document saying that I was to have the *cabildo*;* in those days the house was a Lucumi *cabildo*, because her mother had been a famous priestess of the *santería* religion in Santa Clara. When she died I went to claim the property and this led to a hell of a row. It turned out that her godfather was trying to get his hands on the place. The reason he was doing this was that his woman at the time lived in the place; it was her job to look after the *cabildo*. As soon as I heard what was going on I rushed round and got it all straightened out by some friends of mine in the Provincial Government. I got the house in the end. It was much bigger than I had expected. Not a soul would live in it, especially alone. It was full of spirits and zombies, an accursed place. I sold it to a certain Enrique Obregón, an old man who was a money-lender at high interest. I had a good time with the money, and spent every cent of

* A sort of club created during Spanish rule for African-born slaves and their descendants. Each tribe had its own *cabildo*, dedicated among other things to raising money to fight for Abolition and maintaining tribal traditions. The members used to appear in full tribal regalia on festival days, and this was one of the origins of the National Carnival.

it on flighty women. That was after the war when I was
already getting on a bit.

*

If I count up all the women I had at Ariosa it seems
that I must have had any number of children, but the
strange thing is I never knew of a single one. At least,
none of the women who lived with me in the barracoon
ever had any. The others, the women I took into the
woods, used to come and say, 'This boy is yours,' but
how could you ever be certain with them? Besides,
children were a big problem in those days. You couldn't
educate them because there weren't any schools like
there are now.

When a child was born it had to be taken within three
days of birth to the court-house to be registered. The
first thing they wrote down was the colour of its skin.
Babies were born very easily. The women then didn't
spend as long in labour as they do now, and any old
countrywoman was a better midwife than the trained
people they have now. I never knew of any babies dying
on them. They delivered them with their hands rubbed
with alcohol, and cut their cords, which healed at once.
These old midwives could tell the day and hour when a
woman would give birth. And they did a bit of healing
too. They cured constipation in a flash, with dried dung.
They collected the dung along the road, boiled it, strained
the liquid through a fine cloth, and after two or three
doses the constipation would disappear. They could
cure anything. If a child was suffering from gingivitis
they cured it with forest herbs which they chewed,

boiled and strained and gave to him as an infusion. This killed off the infection at once. The doctors today give different names to these ailments and talk about contagions and eruptions, but when it comes down to it they seem to take twice as long to cure them, even though they had no injections or X-rays in the old days.

All medicines then came from herbs. The whole of Nature is full of cures, any plant has curative powers. The only thing is, many of these haven't been discovered yet. I'd like to know why the doctors don't go into the countryside to experiment with plants. I bet they're too money-minded ever to admit that such-and-such a leaf could cure sickness. Instead they cheat you with bottles of medicine which cost a lot and don't do a body any good. In the old days you couldn't buy medicines like that, so you didn't go to the doctor. A man earning twenty-four pesos a month wasn't going to spend a cent on a bottle of medicine.

I earned twenty-four pesos at Ariosa, although I think there was a time when they were paying me twenty-five, as at Purio. This pay question was flexible, it depended on the way a man worked. I was a good worker, and I was earning as much as twenty-five a month, but there were some poor bastards earning only twenty-four or even eighteen. The pay included food and board in the barracoon, but this didn't impress me much, since this was a life only suited to animals. We lived like pigs, which is one reason why no one wanted to set up home and have children. It was too depressing to think that they would have to endure the same hardships.

There was always a lot going on at Ariosa. Technical advisers constantly came to inspect the fields and the boiler-house, to examine the way the sugar-mill was run and to eliminate errors. Whenever one of these visits was announced, the overseer ordered everyone into clean clothes and the boiler-house was polished up till it shone like the sun. Even the unpleasant smell vanished.

The technical advisers were foreigners. The English and Americans were coming over here even then. The machines had been steam-driven for years. They were small to begin with; later larger ones arrived. The small machines were eventually broken up because they went too slowly and didn't extract all the sap from the sugar-cane. In the old mills half the juice was lost in the *bagasse*. The most important machine was the centrifuge. This had been in use here for something like forty years. I came across it for the first time when I went to Ariosa, but there were still plantations then which didn't have one, like Carmelo, Juanita and San Rafael.

The centrifuge is a round funnel which drains off the syrup and dries the sugar. If a plantation had no centrifuge it could only make *muscovado*, which is a dark brown diluted sugar. The drink they made from this sugar was very good, as nourishing as a steak. The big machine at Ariosa had three rollers, one cutter and two crushing cylinders, each doing a different part of the job. The cutter chopped the cane, the first crusher squeezed out the sap and the second left the *bagasse* dry enough to be taken to the furnaces. The men who worked on these machines were the most favoured people on the plantation; they felt themselves a cut above everyone else and despised the field workers. They called the cane-cutters *cuerós*, which means something like crude or coarse. They were always mocking them. If their hands were calloused they'd say, 'Careful, you might hurt me,' and refuse to shake hands at any price. This attitude did a lot of harm and spread hatred and rows. They even slept apart, machine-minders, sugar-boilers, sugar-masters and weighers—they all had their own houses, comfortable ones too. Some of them were of masonry, though wooden ones with carving round the roof were more usual at Ariosa. Those men behaved foolishly. Later they began to realise that things were changing and tried to be different. But I've always thought the men who worked outside in the sun got the rawest deal of anyone. They worked the hardest and got the worst treatment, and they had to keep to the barracoons at night.

The truth is, progress is an amazing thing. When I saw all those machines moving themselves at once I was astounded. They really seemed to be going by themselves. I had never seen anything to compare with them before. The machines were either English or American, none of them came from Spain. The Spanish didn't know how to make them. The people who were happiest with all these improvements were the smallholders, because the more sugar the boiler-house produced, the more cane the plantation was likely to buy from them.

The smallholders were still new at the game then. They didn't have very large cane-fields—a typical smallholder might have ten or fifteen *besanas*. They often went too far, planting their cane up to the very edge of the sugar-mill town. They didn't have enough land to get rich on in those days. That came later. They were sons-of-bitches too; surlier and meaner even than the big farmers, really miserly about wages and forever shouting at the workers. If there was a piece of land which should have been worth forty pesos, they would pay half for it, and sometimes you were forced to accept a bad price because they got together about this though individually they couldn't stand one another. The workers steered as clear as possible of the smallholders. They didn't speak to them when they went to the fields, and when they collected their wages, they went to the store-keeper for them. It was better that way. The smallholders were too poor to afford overseers in those days. They didn't get the chance to make money till the price of sugar went up, and then some of them rose quite high in the world. The sugar-cane madness came, and in no time at all there was scarcely a forest left in Cuba. They tore the trees up by the roots, they cut down mahogany trees, cedars, indigo-trees, well, almost all the timber. This happened after Independence. Now, if you go to the north of Las Villas you would probably say, 'There are no forests round here,' but when I was a runaway the place was quite frightening, as overgrown as a jungle.

They grew their cane, but they spoiled the beauty of the countryside. The smallholders were the ones to blame. There was hardly a single one who wasn't a mean, stingy bastard, except perhaps Baldomero Bracera. He made a small farm called Juncalito in the marshy part of the Yaguajay valley, and he had the whole place drained in no time at all. This gained him great prestige, and he became very powerful, with more credit even than the owner of the Narcisa plantation, a certain Febles, on whose land Baldomero's farm stood. Febles was a real tyrant; he beat up his workers and then went on behaving towards them as if nothing had happened. He was also very bad about paying wages. One day a worker went up to him and said, 'Pay me.' Febles had him thrown into the furnaces. The man was burnt to a cinder; the only thing left of him was his guts, which was how they discovered the crime. Febles wasn't even touched. As a result, when a man like Baldomero came along, the people loved and respected him. If he had to fire someone he would say so to his face. One of the best things Baldomero did was introduce a cane-hauling machine into Narcisa. Other plantations already had them, but Febles had not been able to afford one because he didn't have enough credit. So Baldomero lent him the money and sent off for one, and a few days later Narcisa had its own cane-hauling machine. I remember it still, because it had this big number painted on one side. Baldomero was a good farmer and a shrewd, clever business man. He gave money to public works and finance and paid fair wages. The village of Yaguajay mourned his death. I never worked for him myself, because that was while I was at Ariosa, but I saw him and I heard lots of stories about him and his rise in the world. Baldomero was the exception to the rule.

People can't imagine how inflammable the country was

during those years. Everyone was constantly talking of rebellion, war was approaching, but I think most people were not sure when it would begin. A lot of them were saying that Spain didn't have much longer to run; the rest kept their mouths shut or hid their heads in a piss-pot. I didn't say anything myself, although I was glad about the revolution and I admired the brave men who were risking their lives for it. The most popular of them were the anarchists, who received their orders from Spain, although they were fighting to free Cuba. They were something like the *náñigos*, very united, and did everything together. They were immensely brave. People were always talking about them. After the war the anarchists became very important in Cuba, but I stopped keeping up with them then. One thing none of us knew about was this annexationism you hear about nowadays. What all of us wanted, as Cubans, was the freedom of Cuba. We wanted the Spanish to go and leave us alone, 'Freedom or Death,' people said, or, 'Free Cuba'.

A lot of people rebelled and got themselves into trouble over this Independence business. They went up into the hills and remained there making a great uproar for several days, and then they either came down again or were taken prisoner. The Civil Guards were hellish bastards, it was dangerous for anyone to get into their bad books. They tore their prisoners to pieces. We Negroes protested too— our grievances went back years—but considering everything, I didn't think Negroes did all that much. I remember the Rosales brothers' rebellion—Panchito and Antonio Rosales. One of them was a journalist and owned a printing press in Sagua la Grande, which was where they both came from. Word went round that the Rosales brothers were breathing fire, attacking the Spanish Government, and this made them popular with the people. I became interested in them myself. I saw Francisco one day as I was passing through Sagua, and as soon as I set eyes on him I realised that this was a man with no belief in anything or anyone. He was elegant and impressive, but he would do you in as soon as look at you. Francisco was a cattle-thief and bandit, though I think he was a barber by profession. I saw both of them once in Rodrigo, they were always going over there—to stir up trouble, naturally. Those mulattoes got too big for their boots. They even passed themselves off as whites. Huh! Antonio was shot in Sagua. The Spanish Government captured him and shot him, and that was the last anyone heard of them. Don't try to tell me those two were revolutionaries. They fought bravely, but they didn't know what they were fighting for. Well, I'm not saying we knew what we were fighting for either, but that didn't make us bandits. The people of Ariosa at least were decent and serious. There was nothing to stop you joining up with the bandits and criminals, but this was a matter of choice and convenience. No one forced any-one else to steal. Evil sticks to evil. I went through the war with a bunch of degenerates, but I came out with my hands clean. Not that the bandits were murderers, however. If someone had to be killed, they killed him, but they weren't really murderers.

*

There were lots of bandits here before the war, some of them very well known. They kept to the countryside, harrying the rich and the small farmers. Manuel García was the most famous. Everyone knew of him, and there were even people who claimed he was a revolutionary. I know of many more besides—Morejón, Machín, Roberto Bermudez and Cayito Alvarez. Cayito was a monster, but as brave as a lion. Anyone in Las Villas could tell you about him. He fought in the war, too. There are a lot of lies going round about him, stories people have made up. Morejón was a wretch. He might steal himself a fortune, but he would never, like Manuel García, use it to buy food for the poor. I never heard of him giving money to the revolution, either. He was always in hiding, he was rather cowardly and cunning, he liked stealing, and he had been a bandit all his life. He took money off people in a straightforward sort of way, without fuss. I don't think he ever kidnapped anyone; instead he stopped people along the road and said, 'Give me everything you've got on you,' then took the cash and disappeared. I never heard of him threatening anyone. On the whole he seemed a quiet sort of fellow, but he was a criminal all the same.

Las Villas was the bandits' centre. There were swarms of them there, kidnappers as well as the ones who seemed to have a knack of getting money out of people without trouble. There were plenty of rich families in the north of Las Villas, and Aguero plundered nearly all of them. He was the biggest thief of the lot. He took everything down to the chickens and pigs and walked out of the place stamping and shouting, so they said. Then everyone chased him and the police cordoned off the area, but he always managed to sneak away. Aguero strolled in and out of the plantations like someone going in and out of his own home. He used disguises a lot; the bandits often passed themselves off as lottery-ticket-sellers, plantation workers and rural policemen. He once came to Ariosa, they say he made a killing there. I didn't see him myself. He wandered slowly into the place, dressed and walking like a police-man, and asked for the owner. They told him at the canteen, 'Keep going uphill, the house isn't far.' When he reached the house—it belonged to a Basque—he asked to be taken to the owner, and they let him through. And then, of course, he drew a gun and demanded a large sum of money. The funny thing is that the owner handed it all over without even guessing that it was Aguero who had robbed him, he was so cleverly disguised and speaking Spanish like a Spaniard. The first thing Aguero had told the Basque to do was dismiss the guards and, like a fool, the man had obeyed.

The evil tongues say that General Maximo Gomez himself took money from Aguero for the rebellion. I can quite believe that. The only one who never accepted any money from bandits was Martí, the patriot of Tampa and the finest man in Cuba.

The civilian population, decent people, were very frightened of the bandits. That is why one of Aguero's friends betrayed him to the police. He was forced to do so because Aguero had gone too far, ransacking plantation after plantation.

*

The most important kidnapping in Remedios was the Falcón case. The Falcóns were one of the strangest families in Las Villas, and they made a hell of a lot of trouble. There was jealousy, hatred and hypocrisy among them, all the emotions which hatch in the minds of heartless people. One of them, Don Miguel Falcón, was penniless. He married a good woman who had no idea of his real character, the widow of the brother of Modesto Ruiz, who was then the village mayor. Her daughters were already quite grown up by the time her husband died, but Don Miguel wanted to marry her all the same, because she was still attractive and young-looking. Everyone called her Antoñica, though her real name was Antonia Romero. Her family was honoured and respected throughout Remedios. Well, what happened was that Don Miguel planned to kidnap Modesto Ruiz during Polavieja's Governorship of the island. Modesto was not a bad fellow, but no one could work out how he came to have so much money. At that time a certain Mendez, a Spaniard, I believe, was Lieutenant-Colonel of the Vueltas volunteers. It was because he knew that Mendez was in Polavieja's confidence that Don Miguel enlisted his help. What Polavieja didn't know was that Mendez was the leader of a gang of bandits, and the most depraved and cruel of the lot.

One day Don Miguel went to see him and said, 'We've got to get those ten thousand pesos out of Modesto.' Mendez said, 'Let's go!' so they and two or three others arranged to seize Modesto on one of his trips to his farm, La Panchita. When they had carried out this plan, they took him to the forest and forced him to tell them where he kept his money. Of course Don Miguel took care not to show himself while all this was going on, in case Modesto recognised him. I believe Modesto was kept a prisoner for almost two weeks by Mendez's bloodthirsty crew. He confessed about the money at once, and they seized it all and left him locked up in a house, with his feet bound. A little later they ordered one of the bandits, a mulatto, to go and kill him and bury him deep in the ground. The mulatto went to Modesto and they talked and Modesto kept saying, 'Set me free and I will see that you are rewarded.' The mulatto, feeling sorry for him, said, 'I will set you free if you promise to get me out of Cuba safely.' Modesto promised, and the mulatto freed him. Soon afterwards Don Miguel Falcón heard what had happened, and he pretended to be delighted and organised a big party for Modesto at his home. Modesto went to it, and everyone made a great fuss of him. But he felt the Devil's hand in all this and told himself that the affair was not going to end there.

He began making enquiries, and as soon as he had all the proof he needed, he went to Polavieja. By now Mendez, the murderer, had had the mulatto killed; there never had been the smallest chance of his escaping from Cuba. Polavieja, who disliked the bandits, had Mendez arrested and court-martialled. He was shot in Havana. Don Miguel was seized a few days later and deported to Ceuta, which is an island surrounded by devils, and died there not long after. By now the truth was out, and everyone was astounded. Nobody had guessed what those bandits were up to. Poor Antonia was struck dumb, especially when she found that her own husband had plotted to kill her brother-in-law so that her daughters should come into his money, not to mention the ten thousand pesos they had planned to share out among themselves. I don't know whether they caught the rest of the gang, but I think it's unlikely, because the rural police weren't as sharp then as they are now. They were a bloodthirsty lot, but stupid. Antonia Romero was a fine woman. She was ashamed of what had happened, but she didn't let it break her spirit. Nor did her daughters. When the war began Antonia collaborated with the revolutionaries and made clothes, cooked and distributed medicines. Later she went to fight in the forest and rose to the rank of lieutenant-colonel in the revolutionary army.

*

Some people like to make out that the bandits were benefactors and good men, because they stole to give to the poor. Well, it seems to me that robbery, however you look at it, is still robbery. And the bandits were not too fussy about whom they plundered. Rich or middling rich was all the same to them. All they cared about was having cash in their pockets, and certainly this was one thing they never lacked. Though sometimes they were forced to take shelter in the *guajiros*' homes and eat a dish of sweet potato so as not to go hungry. That is where this idea of the benevolent bandits comes from; obviously if the *guajiros* offered them their hospitality they had to repay them somehow, so whenever they stole a large sum of money they shared it with them. Naturally the *guajiros* became great friends of the bandits, even though they didn't become bandits themselves. Those *guajiros* have always been obliging types. If they saw a bandit riding up on horseback, the wife would say, 'Come and have a cup of coffee with us,' and the bandit would dismount and take advantage of their kindness to make friends with all the family. The very same bandits would often make off with the *guajiros*' daughters, in fact this was the most usual sort of kidnapping. I have never known men as women-crazy as those damned bandits. They would risk their lives to see a woman. The police got wind of the visits they paid to certain women and ambushed them on the spot. They hunted down a lot of bandits this way because it was useless trying to catch them out in the open country— they were bold as lynxes, and the best horsemen anywhere, and they knew the forest like the back of their hands. Many of them claimed they were revolutionaries who wanted Cuba to be free, but they only did this for show. Murderers don't turn into patriots. What they did like was setting fire to things. They would go to some farmer and say, 'Come on, where's the money?' and if the farmer refused to give them any, they threatened to fire his fields. They weren't joking either. From time to time you would see fires raging, and it was all their doing.

They usually made their raids at night; that was when they committed their crimes. The days they spent resting. It was a dangerous life, because the Spanish Government hated them. The whole island was getting infested with them; they could be found in all the provinces.

The most popular of them was Manuel García, whom they still call the King of the Cuban Countryside. They even talk about him on the radio. I never saw him myself, but I know that he roamed about all over the place. People tell lots of stories about him.

Manuel never lost an opportunity. Wherever he saw there was money to be had, he moved in to snatch it. This boldness of his won him many friends and many enemies, but I think more enemies than friends. They say he wasn't a murderer. I don't know about that, but one thing I'm sure about is that he had a very lucky guardian angel. Everything turned out well for him. He was a friend of the *guajiros*, a real friend. If they ever saw the police getting close to a place where Manuel was, they used to take their trousers off and hang them on a rope waist down. This was the signal for Manuel to get moving, and that must be why he lived for so long as an outlaw.

He was the most daring of all the bandits. He would as soon stop a train as derail it. He collected protection money. Oh, and much more . . . With Manuel it got to the point where he didn't even bother to cut the telegraph wires, because he felt so certain that no one would ever capture him. Polavieja and Salamanca fought harder against him than anyone else. And another general who came here, called Lachambre, was convinced he was going to capture him. All Manuel did was laugh at him and send him letters threatening to hang him. Lachambre was brave enough, but he never managed to lay hands on Manuel, even though the Spanish had better arms and more men. Manuel's gang used rifles which fired eighteen rounds, good weapons compared with the blunderbusses used by the other bandits. It was a well supplied gang; they had cooks, orderlies and so on, and they never went short of tobacco, hot chocolate, vegetables or pork.

Manuel García cut a big dash in Cuba, especially in Havana. He enjoyed his way of life, and he wasn't ashamed to say so. He started off as a cattle-thief in the countryside, stealing cattle to sell, then he moved on to robbing and kidnapping. I believe he was born in Quivicán, and it was there he married Rosario, who was his only wife. She was imprisoned on Pine Island and everybody gossiped about this. Vicente García, Manuel's brother, was a bandit too, but not so famous. I heard much talk about Osma, Manuel's right-hand man, a stubborn, rebellious Negro who later joined the Guerillas of Death* and fought with them all over the place. There were lots of them in Las Villas. Osma killed at point-blank range with a great blunderbuss of brass and wood. People talked of him as though he were a witch. I'm not sure about that, but he must have had some sort of power, because for that band to travel the distances it did some *Regla de Palo*† magic must have been needed.

* The name of a Cuban battalion which fought on the Spanish side in the War of Independence. Esteban always uses the word 'guerillas' to mean Cubans who fought for Spain, and so traitors in his eyes.

† Literally 'Cult of the Stick', a religion of Congolese origin mixed with animist and Catholic elements. It was less sophisticated than *santería* and concentrated on magic.

Manuel García never actually fought in the War of Independence, though he contributed a lot of money towards it, something like fifty thousand pesos, which General Maximo Gomez accepted like manna from heaven. Manuel's death remains a mystery. When a man is as famous as that, it is hard to get to the truth. He had lots of enemies, because all the families he crossed were after him. Once he kidnapped a certain Hoyo whose relations pursued him ever after, without success, for Manuel knew every inch of the forest.

I have often heard, from the old men who knew him personally, that it was women who destroyed him in the end. I am convinced myself that he was killed for having given money to the revolution. A traitor passing himself off as a revolutionary arranged to meet him in the forest and told him to light up a cigarette so that he would be recognised. Manuel, trusting him, turned up at the meeting-place as he had promised, carrying thousands of pesos on him. As soon as he came near, the traitor called to the police to shoot and they made a sieve of him. This is how I believe Manuel García died.

But other people tell a different story. In the west of Cuba they say Manuel was killed because he went to see a girl in Mocha. He used to have her every night. Then one day this stupid cow went to the village priest and said, 'Ay, Father, I am sleeping with Manuel García!' and the priest informed on her to the authorities. A few days later when Manuel García went to her house he opened the swing-gate and left it that way. When he came out soon afterwards the gate was shut, and this struck him as strange. When he went to open it they shouted to him, 'Manuel García!' He looked round, and the Civil Guard shot him down on the spot.

I have heard still another version of the story: that a sacristan from the parish of Canasí killed him in a tavern and that García's men later killed the sacristan with machetes in the forest. But it's all a bit dark, no one can say what really happened. It's the same with General Maceo's death—there's something fishy about it. People find it hard to speak out straight. That's why I say that although the magic-men may be witches and all that, at least they don't hush up the truth. They tell you who your enemy is and how to get rid of him. They were the only people who spoke out openly at Ariosa, and if you paid them they told you more. A lot of people were afraid of them. People started saying that they ate babies and tore out their hearts and a heap of stinking lies, but when you hear things like that you shouldn't be frightened, you should make sure of the facts first. People only talk like that when something is biting them.

I don't support witchcraft, but I don't say stupid things for fun either. I am more frightened of other things than I am of witchcraft. I wasn't even afraid of the bandits. The point is, I was poor, skint, and nobody was likely to kidnap me, however far I walked, and I used to walk till I was tired out.

The forest is a tiring place to be in all the time, especially if you are working from dawn to dusk, because the sun is shut out by the trees. When I worked in the cane-fields, the sun went through my shirt and warmed me inside. The heat was good. I used to sweat all over there. All the same, the sun looks grander somehow when you are out walking, and it is cooler, or seems like it.

But to go back to this thing of being afraid. It's silly to be frightened of witches or bandits. Much more dangerous, as everyone agreed, were the Spanish military and the local captains. I remember when I was at Ariosa there was one little captain who was the bloody end, I don't remember his name, but anyway he got my goat without my knowing it. 'Here comes the Captain' was much the same as saying, 'Here comes the Devil.' Everyone avoided the captains. If they smelt trouble brewing or even caught a whiff of it, they were down on you. When the Negroes started rebelling against Spain, the captains had a good time. A Negro revolutionary was something which couldn't be allowed to exist! They shot them at once. On the other hand, if the man was white, well . . . I know it's better not to think about that time. There's nothing worse than getting a thrashing from some arrogant Spanish swine if you have to keep your mouth shut!

Anyone who put a foot wrong was sent to clean out the Civil Guard stables. The Civil Guard always went about on horseback, although there were some who did their service in the infantry. The mounted ones were the toughest of the lot. They didn't have any small, weakly men in the Civil Guard, no sir, and they didn't have any good ones either. They were bastards, the lot of them. The only reason they lasted so long is that there weren't many rebellious men then, not like now. In those days a revolutionary was a rare thing. People were too long-suffering by half. No one would have dared defy a captain, they would sooner have died.

There was one red-haired Negro who did make a name for himself in Cuba, though. His name was Tajó, and he lived in Sapo. Once he disarmed two pairs of Civil Guards at the same time. He had been regularly breaking the law, living as an outlaw and robbing people, until the war began. Tajó was a wicked devil. If he took a fancy to a woman, he made off with her and woe betide anyone who complained. If it happened that the woman's father came to fetch her back, he would brandish his machete to frighten him and the poor man would run away. That shows you the sort of bastard he was. He always got what he wanted. He even slept with his own daughters. Everyone knew about this, though they did nothing about it. The poor daughters spent their lives shut up in the house and weren't allowed out, even to sit in the sun. They looked like ghosts from having been cooped up for so long. The people in the farms around had no idea what they looked like or whether they were pretty or ugly—he wanted them for his own pleasure and nothing else. I never saw these girls, but I know this is true for certain, because everyone talked about it and news came to Ariosa like spray on the wind. Some people even said that after Tajó had slept with the local village women he used to kill them and bury their bodies in an ant-heap, but this was an exaggeration, although I would be prepared to believe almost anything of that

[124]

bugger. All his tastes were criminal; he was the sort of man who never thought of simply having a good time or playing games, only of doing harm. In the war I found myself under his command. It was the fault of Maximo Gómez, who put him in charge of a platoon.

But to get back to women; they were certainly the big topic of conversation. You might go along to chat to your friends, or rather your acquaintances, and they would begin telling you all the things they did with women. I wasn't given to talking about my own experiences. A man should learn to keep certain things to himself. But these big-mouths would tell you quite calmly, 'I say, So-and-So, I'm going to make out with What's-her-name tomorrow.' When they talked to me like that, I used to pretend I hadn't heard so as to keep a distance between us. I don't like that sort of gossip. I prefer to stick to gambling games which are a healthier pastime.

There were some good domino-players at Ariosa. Dominoes is a difficult game to play, you need to keep a clear head. We played many different kinds, especially *la convidada* and tin-tin-tin, where you keep your spots hidden. If the Civil Guard caught you playing they thrashed you within an inch of your life. I used to get bored with all this domino-playing after a bit and wander off to listen to the elders and the young men talking about their visions.

All men have their visions, and most of them keep quiet about them. I believe in visions myself, and I think they should be respected, not feared. I have seen many different ones myself and I still remember some of them. Other people have told me about theirs, like the friend of mine who saw fire coming out of his right arm. This was bad; if it had come from his left arm, it would have meant he was about to die. There are people who spend all their time thinking about visions and waiting entranced for one to appear. Then, of course, they never do, and as a result many people don't believe in them at all.

People who have the gift of visions see them almost every day; people who don't can still see them from time to time, though less often. I wouldn't call myself a seer, though I have seen strange things, like a light which walked alongside me and kept stopping when it came to a place where there was buried money to be dug up, and then disappeared. This was a dead person who had come up to get money. Other spirits used to appear as lights, but what they were after was candles. They would stick by my side as I was walking along, and without them saying a word I knew what they wanted was for me to pay for a candle for them in the church. I never did, and the lights used to keep on appearing to me. They don't appear now because I don't get about as much as I did, and the lights are a country thing.

Another vision people had was the *guijes*, little black men with men's hands and feet like . . . well, I never found out what sort of feet they had, but their heads were flattened like frogs', exactly like frogs'. Ave Maria, the fuss and commotion there was when the *guijes* appeared! Negroes had a natural tendency to see them.

[126]

They would come up out of the river at all hours, and if they heard you coming they crept under the banks and hid themselves. They used to come out to take the sun. Mermaids were yet another vision. They used to appear at sea, especially on San Juan's day. They came up to comb their hair and look for men—they are all great flirts. There have been many cases of mermaids stealing men away and taking them down under the sea, fishermen especially. They let them go again after keeping them down there for a while. I don't know what magic they used to stop them drowning. This is one of the strange things of life, one of the mysteries.

Witches are another of these mysteries. I once saw one of them captured at Ariosa. It was done with sesame- and mustard-seed. If there is so much as a single sesame-seed on the ground, a witch is rooted to the spot and can't move an inch. When witches appeared they took off their skins and hung them up behind the door and stepped out just like that, all raw. There aren't many of them left here, because the Civil Guard exterminated them all. They were all Canary Islanders, I never saw a single Cuban witch. They flew across here every night, covering the distance from the Canaries to Havana in a few minutes. People are not so frightened of these things as they were, but I notice they still leave lights burning in houses where there are small children to keep the witches out. Just as well, because witches are very fond of infants.

The headless rider is another common apparition. They ride out to atone for their sins and they are a terrifying sight. I met one once, and he said, 'Come here and dig up this treasure.' I was shivering with fright, and when I dug all I found was coal. It must have been a dead joker who had been buried without a cross. I never saw him again. Those spooks were amazing. They say the dead are bigger bastards than the living, and there may be something in it, for all I know.

The plantation was full of witchcraft. The Filipinos were always meddling in this sort of thing, stirring up the Negroes and even sleeping with Negresses. They were a bunch of crooks. If one of them died they would bury him near a Negro, and soon afterwards he would appear dressed in red and scare the wits out of everybody. The old men tended to see these apparitions more than the young ones, who hardly ever did. A young man does not have the gift of seeing much, and he rarely hears voices either, country voices. You could be walking along a country road at night and hear a cry or a snore. I was used to this happening, and I wasn't very frightened. Right here in Santa Clara they used to say you could hear snoring noises in the Alvarez's pigsties at night. Well, that's what they told me: I never saw those particular ghosts. I have always believed, though not everyone agrees with me, that these ghosts are spirits who died owing something, a mass or a prayer. As soon as they have carried out their mission they vanish again.

All this is to do with the spirit world, and we should face it without fear. The living are more dangerous. I never heard of so-and-so's spirit beating anyone up, but think of all the live people tearing each other's hair out all day long! That's the way to look at it, fairly and squarely. If a dead person comes up to you, don't run away, ask him, 'What do you want, brother?' He will either answer or take you away with him somewhere. Never turn your face away from them; after all, you can't say the dead are enemies, exactly.

In the old days people really were afraid of the dead. Even the Chinese got scared and opened their slit eyes; their skin went quite pasty whenever one of their countrymen died. A man had only to lie down and the Chinese would scurry away and leave him on his own, quite alone. Several hours later they would all get together and find some Cuban to lay out the corpse and bury it. The dead man did not complain, of course. How could he? Then they would all go to the dead man's room, and I could swear they were cooking in there, because the most delicious smell used to come out, and it wasn't opium. I can't imagine why they were so frightened, it's impossible to explain.

The Congolese were different, they weren't afraid of the dead. They would put on serious faces, but they weren't frightened. There was no weeping when a Congolese died, only a great deal of praying and singing in a low voice, without the drums. Then they would take the dead man to the cemetery, which was next to the plantation, and bury him there just as he was, without a coffin: they didn't use coffins. I think myself that it must be better to be buried like that and not shut up in a box, unable to do anything in all that darkness. They left a little mound on top of the grave and set a cedar-wood cross on top of it to protect the dead Negro. The Congolese said that the corpses should not have their eyes open, so they stuck them down with sperm, which kept them tight shut. If the eyes opened again it was a bad sign. Also, they always buried the dead face upwards, I don't know why, but I suppose because it was the custom. They were dressed in all their clothes, right down to their shoes. If the dead man had been a priest of the Cult of the Stick he would have left his magic pot to someone, because when one of the sect fell ill he always chose another member to bequeath it to. But if that person was unable to take it on, he had to throw it into the river for the current to wash away, because if you didn't understand how to treat a shrine which had been bequeathed to you, it could screw up your whole life. Those magic pots were hellishly tricky, they could easily kill you.

To make a magic pot which works well you need to collect stones, sticks and bones; these are the essential things. When there was a flash of lightning the Congolese used to mark the spot where it struck, wait seven years and then go to the place and dig about till they found a smooth stone for the magic pot. The buzzard's stone was good strong magic too, but you had to be ready for the moment when the buzzard went to lay her eggs. She always laid two, and one of these had to be taken carefully away and cooked, and then put back in the nest till the other egg hatched. Then the cooked egg would wait for the buzzard to go to the sea because she believed the remaining egg would hatch out too. She fetched a magic charm from the sea, a little rough pebble, which she laid beside the egg still in the nest. The stone contained such powerful magic

that in a few hours the cooked egg would hatch out too. This
is the honest truth. A magic pot which was prepared
with this little stone could not be trifled with or inherited
by just anyone. That is why the Congolese died so sadly.

*

Some people said that when a Negro died he went back
to Africa, but this is a lie. How could a dead man go to
Africa? It was living men who flew there, from a tribe
the Spanish stopped importing as slaves because so
many of them flew away that it was bad for business.
Holy Moses, dead men don't fly! The Chinese who died
here, so they said, came to life again in Canton. But
with the Negroes, what happened was that their spirits
left their bodies and wandered about over the sea
and through space, like when a snail leaves its shell and
goes into another and then another and another. That's
why there are so many shells. The dead don't appear as
corpses but as spirit shapes. There was one who used
to appear at Ariosa called Faustino Congo. He swilled
up alcohol like an animal. He came because he had money
buried round the place in jars. They buried money like
that in those days; there were no banks. Two Spaniards
were digging one day and found the buried money and got
rich. Faustino never appeared again; probably he'd only
come to keep an eye on his money. Apparently the two
Spaniards were his friends and he wanted them to have
the money. They left a lot of coins scattered about, and
everyone rushed to grab them. The Spaniards ran away,
so as not to have to give half the treasure to the Government. People forgot about Faustino once he stopped

appearing, but I still remember him clearly. I try not to think too much about all this, though, because it is too tiring.

Thinking is tiring. Even now there are people who don't believe the dead walk, or anything like that, simply because they haven't seen it happen. If the young don't believe, it's because they haven't seen these things. They get just as tired, though, thinking about modern problems, the peoples of the world, wars and so on. They waste their time like that, and don't have any fun. Others plunge themselves into vice and trickery, and what with that and the way of thinking they have got into, their life just fritters away. You can tell them this, but they don't take any notice. They don't believe you, they don't even listen.

I once told a young man about the little devil, and he said I was lying. Well, it may sound like a lie, but it's the plain truth. A man can make his own little devil, yes sir, he can. An old Congolese from the Timbirito plantation showed me how to do it. He spent hours talking to me, telling me I should learn to do stick magic because I was serious and quiet. You should have heard his stories. He had seen it all, everything down here below and up above too. He was a bit cantankerous, really, but I got on all right with him. I never said, 'You don't know what you're talking about' or laughed at him. The old fellow was like a father to me. Well, to get back to the little devil. He showed me how to make one. I was on my way through Timbirito one day and he saw me sitting alone and started talking to me. 'Creole, come with me,' he said, 'I want to show you something.' I thought it would be money, or perhaps a charm like the ones the Congolese wore, but it was nothing like that. He rambled on in this mysterious sort of way, 'You're a fool, Creole,' and he showed me a bottle he took from his pocket. 'Look, see this, with this you can do all you want.' I realised then that he was talking about magic. I learnt to make a little devil, care for it and everything. It takes a lot of guts to do this, and a heart as cool as a fish's. It isn't difficult. You get an egg with a chick in it—it has to have a chick or it won't work—and you put it out in the sun for two or three days. When it's hot you hold it in your armpit on three Fridays, one after the other, and on the third Friday instead of a chicken a little devil will hatch out, the colour of a chameleon. Then you put this little devil into a little transparent glass bottle and feed it dry wine and keep it in your trouser pocket, taking good care that it doesn't get away, because those little devils are fierce creatures and wriggle their tails about the whole time. With one of those you can do what you want. But of course you musn't expect to get it all at one go, you have to go about things gradually. Some time later during the year you will have to get rid of the little devil because you have done enough with it by then; then you must take it down to the river at night and throw it in so the current carries it away. One thing, though: the man who does this magic will never be able to cross that river again. He can try to cross it twenty times, but each time a great harm will come to him.

The best time for this sort of magic is a Tuesday, or

so they say. When a magic-man wants to do stick magic, especially black stick magic, he always does it on a Tuesday because that's the Devil's day, an evil day. Apparently the Devil had to choose himself a day, and he picked that one. To tell you the truth, every time I hear that word, Tuesday, nothing more, just Tuesday, I bristle inwardly and I feel the Devil there in person. If the magic-men wanted to prepare a magic pot for black magic, they did it on a Tuesday because that made it stronger. It was prepared with beef, Christian bones, especially ankle-bones, which are good for black magic. Then they took the pot to an ant-heap and buried it there, again on a Tuesday. They left it in the ant-heap two or three weeks, then one Tuesday they dug it up again and that was when they made the pact, which meant saying to the shrine, 'I will do evil, I will do what you want.' This oath was sworn at midnight, the Devil's hour, and it bound the Congolese to a pact with the Devil, or *Endoquí*, as the Congolese call him. This oath wasn't a game or a joke; if you didn't carry it out faithfully, you could die suddenly. A lot of people who die like this, without having been ill, are being punished by the Devil. After swearing the oath and digging up the pot, the Congolese would take it home and stand it in a corner and feed it the other ingredients: Guinea pepper, garlic, pods from the *guaguao*-tree, a skull and one more ankle-bone, all wrapped in a black cloth. The cloth, with the things inside it, was placed on top of the pot, and . . . watch out, anyone who looked inside! The pot couldn't do anything till it had these extra things, but after that it was powerful

[134]

enough to scare off the Devil himself. There was nothing it couldn't manage. The pot also held a thunder-stone and a buzzard-stone, which are both strong black magic.

I saw many things done with these pots, terrible things —people killed, trains derailed, houses set fire to, and much more besides. . . . When you hear people talk of black magic you should keep calm and respectful, because respect opens every door. That was how I learned about these things.

This Congolese from Timbirito told me a lot about his meetings with the Devil. He saw him as often as he wanted. I think the Devil is a smart fellow; he obeys when people summon him so as to work evil and give himself pleasure. But don't try calling him for some good purpose because p-h-h-t! he won't come! If a person wants to make a pact with him, the old Congolese told me, he should take a hammer and a big nail, look for a young *ceiba*-tree in the countryside and hammer on the trunk hard three times. As soon as the bugger hears this call, he comes, quite cool and cocky, as if he didn't care a damn. He sometimes appears dressed very smartly like a man but never as a devil, for he doesn't want to frighten people. In his natural shape he is all red like a flame, with fire coming from his mouth and a pitchfork in one hand. When he appears you can speak to him quite normally, but you have to make your meaning very clear because to him years are just days, and if you promise to do something in three years he will think you said three days. If you don't know this, you are in trouble—I've known it ever since I was a slave. The Devil reckons things up in quite a different way from men. He loves doing wickedness. I don't know what he's like now, but he used to give all the help he could, so that spells would work.

Anyone could summon up. A lot of aristocrats, counts and marquises, had dealings with him. Also Masons, and even Christians. I never had much time for this Freemasonry, because wherever there is secrecy you will find witchcraft, and the Masons are very secretive. I am sure the Devil enters into their religion too. They learnt about the Congolese Devil from the Congolese elders. The elders showed the counts and the marquises how to do stick magic, and told them, 'When you do *mayombe* you are lords of the earth.' The counts and marquises did as the elders commanded, collecting earth from four corners, wrapping it in corn straw and making four little mounds, each with a chicken's foot tied to it. Then they offered all this to the magic pot so as to get their wishes. If anything went wrong in the preparation, they broke up the pot by hitting it with broomsticks and took to their heels. Those pots acquired tremendous power, and they could suddenly turn it against you.

*

The Congolese used many types of good-luck charms. A little stick or a bone were both good ones. I used some of them while I was at Ariosa and during the war as well. The one I had then helped me a lot and often saved me from getting killed. I was wounded once, but it was only a flesh wound, which they cured with camphor.

[136]

The best charms are made with pebbles. All you have to do is fill a little leather bag with them and hang it round your neck, but the important thing is never to neglect it. The bag needs to be fed from time to time, just like a person, and the food is chosen by the lord of the magic pot, who is the one who gives out the charms; usually it is garlic and pods of the *guaguao*-tree, also a little alcohol to drink, and an occasional pinch of Guinea pepper. When one of the Negro magic-men gave out a lucky charm, he would stare hard at you for a moment, clap your hands between his, squeeze them hard, and make you promise that you would not put it to any evil use and that you would go without sex of any kind while you were wearing it.

These charms are tricky things. If a man tries to sleep with a woman while he is wearing one, he will flop, and the charm will bring him bad luck for a long time. Besides, women weaken the magic. If you want to put it on again after sex, you must first scrub your hands with ashes to placate the evil spirits, otherwise the charm will turn against you.

Women weaken everything from charms to magic pots, which is why they have their own forms of magic. They can be witches too, but they don't work with the men's pots. Some women are more powerful and bold with magic than men, but I think they are best at purifying and cooling magic, especially cooling.

I don't remember which woman it was that taught me about kerosene cans, but I know it was many years ago. It's the best cooling thing there is. All you do is take a big kerosene can and fill it with water and herbs, the sort of herbs you find in rich people's gardens, like sweet basil, *apasote* and nut-pine, and a little sugar and salt. Then you put the can in a corner for two days, after which you sprinkle the water all over the house. It stinks a bit, but it does make the place cooler; after a little while you feel soft, cool air blowing in through the doors, and it is very health-giving. You can bathe in the water, too, but without the salt and sugar. The baths should be taken at midday when the sun is directly overhead, and seven baths are sufficient for purification. In the old days people had these baths daily; the Congolese claimed that they were good for health, and the practice was called *gangulería*, witchcraft, though people said it was spiritualism.

Spirits are less powerful than witchcraft. I didn't take much notice of what the elders told me, I just went along with a bit of it so as not to offend them. Men like me are not much given to witchcraft because we are not patient enough. I was fond of mischief and teasing, and this doesn't go with witchcraft. I liked to see and hear things for myself, so as to make up my own mind, and I couldn't stand being told that I mustn't touch or know about something. If that happened I lost my temper and carried on in my own way.

I once did a naughty thing, which I can't think about without feeling scared. Really scared! What happened is that I went along to this *santero*'s house and started examining all the rooms, cupboards, everything. The *santero* saw me and didn't say anything. Then I decided to go into the last room, the one where they keep the drums and white cloths and tureens, and the saints themselves. I treated myself to a banquet in there, bananas, little sweet cakes made of syrup and grated coconut, all the food put out for the saints. When I was stuffed full, I came out and ran into the *santero*, who looked at me and asked, 'What's the matter?' I didn't answer and he passed by, but this remark of his must have made my legs shake, for they shook and shook as though I were ill. Well, of course I had to run. But the point is, there was no reason for this shaking, because it wasn't as if the *santero* had caught me; if he had caught me it would have been different. You aren't supposed even to touch the saints' food, but when a man is hungry he loses his grip on himself. The Congolese themselves would never have done such a thing, even as a joke. If one of them caught you sticking your nose where it didn't belong, you had to watch out, they might even get their black magic to work on you! The Congolese are more daring and hard-headed than the Lucumis. They work their magic with objects; it is all based on sticks, bones, blood, forest trees.

A tree is very important to a Congolese, because everything comes from it and is to be found in it. It is like a god; they feed it and talk to it and ask things of it and look after it. Everything they do is with the help of Nature, especially the tree, which is the soul of Nature. Witchcraft makes use of trees and herbs. There were thickets and good-sized trees on all the plantations during slavery, which were ideal places for the Congolese magic-men. At Ariosa, too, there were large fields and wooded places where witchcraft flourished. They used to make spirits and lights appear along with a whole lot of other things which I am beginning to forget with the years, things you can't put words to, mysteries in fact. The most impressive thing I ever saw in my life was the Congolese elders changing themselves into animals. Now that was extraordinary!

They did such wicked things sometimes, it made your hair stand on end and your flesh creep. They might tell you that so-and-so was going to come out of the compound in the shape of a cat or a dog, and immediately a Negress would rush out tearing her hair and screaming, 'Help, help, I've just seen a dog the size of my husband!' And the dog might well be the husband in person, in the person of the dog, that is.

I don't recall seeing this myself, but it was frightening enough just to hear the stories, and people spent the whole time telling stories in those days. The idea that a mad dog was really some wicked old Congolese was enough to make your blood run cold. This sort of thing seems to have died out in Cuba, at least I have not heard any more accounts of it. I think maybe the reason it happened here was that there were so many Africans. There aren't any Africans in Cuba now, and the new people couldn't care less about religion, all they think about is eating and sleeping and having lots of money to throw around. That's why we're in this state, wars here, wars there. People need faith, they have to believe in something; if we didn't we would all be up shit creek.

[140]

A man who doesn't believe in miracles today may come to believe in them tomorrow. Proofs occur every day, some more convincing than others, but all quite reasonable. There are times when a man gets over-confident and loses his head, and this leads to disillusionment. At such times there seem to be no saints or miracles or any damn thing, but they soon pass, for a man lives and thinks best in tranquillity.

When you feel all hot inside, as if there was a swelling in there, and too tongue-tied even to open your mouth, you can't think at all, or if you do, only bad thoughts. This can be dangerous. It's sensible to keep some cool water standing near at times like these. In two or three weeks it will cool the whole atmosphere. Cool water is very good. I am sure it clears the mind, and it seems to purify the air without getting all used up. If the water starts to run dry, you may have to fill up the glass, but this means the water is doing its work well. In the barracoons every one had their little jar of water and herbs hanging on the wall. They weren't fools. I never saw inside the boss's homes, but I am sure they had their own things because they were certainly believers.

In this country Catholicism always seems to get mixed up with magic somewhere along the way. This is a fact. There is no such thing as a Catholic pure and simple. The rich people were Catholics, but they also paid heed to witchcraft from time to time. And the overseers were really impressed by it, they didn't dare take their eyes off the Negro magic-men for a second, because they knew that if the Negroes wanted they could split their skulls open. Lots of people here tell you they are Catholic and Apostolic. I don't believe a word of it! Here almost everyone has their little missal and their stick. No person is one thing pure and simple in this country, because all the religions have got mixed together. The African brought his, which is the stronger one, and the Spaniard brought his, which isn't so strong, but you should respect them all. That is my way of thinking.

*

The African religions are more entertaining because you dance, sing, amuse yourself, fight. There is the *maní* dance, the stick game, and *quimbumbia*. At sunset the various groups got together to play *quimbumbia*, which was like witchcraft, and they almost always used drums as in the stick game. *Quimbumbia* was a Congolese thing. At one time two teams of magic-men used to compete with each other. First they planted a plantain-tree in the middle of a circle drawn on the ground, and then each magic-man cast a spell on the plantain-tree to make it grow fruit. They would pass in front of it, kneel, squirt two or three mouthfuls of alcohol over it, and the first one to make it grow fruit was the winner. The winner could eat the bananas or share them out among his team, if he liked.

Afterwards they played the drums and danced to celebrate. The winner was called 'the cock', and the others cheered him on to dance. Whenever these groups wanted to play *quimbumbia* they got handfuls of magic sticks from the forest and tied them in bundles of five, to give each man strength. But I don't rate *quimbumbia* as bad black magic. There was another game which was really fierce, where they plucked a live cockerel, killed it and took all the innards and feathers to a big cooking-pot. When the bird was cooked, they ate it and threw the bones back into the pot, because cock's bones are the strongest magic of all.

That business of eating the cockerel was a good joke to play on a Christian, because after everyone had chewed and swallowed the bird, it would suddenly jump out of the pot when you least expected it. It would step out in the middle of all the noise and excitement, looking quite whole and unharmed. And so it was.

Quimbumbia was played on Tuesdays because it was black magic. The same cockerel would be used in twenty magic ceremonies, because it had proved itself very strong. *Quimbumbia* was almost always played at night. There was no electricity then, of course, and all the plantations were lit by kerosene lamps. They used these to light the *quimbumbia* ceremony too, although darkness is good for witchcraft; spirits don't come where there is light, they are like albinos who can only see in the dark.

The first place they had electricity was Santa Clara, in the town itself. Marta Abreu, the great benefactress, had it sent there, but they didn't get it at Ariosa till . . . well, I don't remember exactly, but it was after they had it in Caracas. Caracas introduced electricity to the Lajas region and was the biggest plantation in Cuba. The owners were millionaires, which is how they were able to buy the light. Their name was Terry. I suppose I must have climbed up a tree or a roof somewhere to get my first look at the lights. I remember that they were dazzling.

In the barracoon I used kerosene lamps, which they sold in the store. I imagine the other plantation-owners must have been a bit envious of all that splendour and luxury at Caracas. Those Terrys were aristocrats, very elegant people who went to France every year. The oldest of them was Don Tomás Terry. I often saw him at a distance. He was a man with ideas ahead of this time. His son, Emilio, was the same, but Don Tomás was the best of the lot. All the workers liked him. He made friends with the Congolese Negroes and gave them quite a bit of help. He even gave money for the blacks to found their *cabildos* with, and he treated them well. They say he used to enjoy watching their dances. There was a Congolese *cabildo* founded by Don Tomás in Cruces and another in Lajas, both of which I visited. I went to find women, because all the pretty black girls went there. But anyone who behaved coarsely got thrown out on his ear. Those black women soon put a man in his place.

I remember they had a photograph of Don Tomás Terry in the *cabildo* at Cruces. I wish all the slave-owners had been like him and his sons! I don't know what happened to them, but I imagine they must be in France living it up like the millionaires that they are.

Ariosa plantation was different, not poor by any means but without the elegance and comfort of Caracas. The sugar-mill town was lit by big gas lamps, as was the whole sugar plant during the sugar-making season—the rest of the time it was as black as pitch. They always left one little light burning at the gate of the barracoon, but that was all. No wonder the men got bored and thought about nothing but women. Women were and are my own obsession. I still think they are the best thing in life. You should have seen me when there was a woman I fancied, I was a devil then, not wild but ready for anything. The women of Remedios were famous for their looks; the best way to get to see them was by going to the fiestas held there every year. I must have been to at least ten, and I saw every girl in the place. Those fiestas were religious feast-days and public festivals both at once, perhaps more religious than the other, but all fiestas have their entertainments, otherwise they wouldn't be fiestas. But they were very serious about religion at Remedios, it was a pious, respectable sort of place. All the houses had altars with figures of male and female saints on them, some pretty, some ugly. Remedios was famous for having good fiestas in Holy Week. Most of the week the people went about dressed in black, keeping very solemn and quiet. No one was allowed to come into the village on horseback, let alone wearing spurs, because those were days of penitence. Even the trains weren't allowed to whistle. It was all as quiet as the grave. On Maundy Thursday people were forbidden to sweep out their homes because the whites said this was like sweeping God's head, and you weren't supposed to wash in water because it might turn to blood. What a silly idea! No pigs or chickens were killed; it was a period of mourning for the whites; they said anyone who ate meat was a sinner and ought to be punished. I saw lots of country people gorging on roast pork, though.

[145]

There were many strange customs at Remedios, particularly in Holy Week. I got to know them all fairly well because I liked the place and often went there. Some of them spread as far as Ariosa. I remember one custom which obliged first cousins who married to pay a forfeit to God. Marriages between first cousins were not approved of, so they had to pay up so as not to be guilty of sin. This system was nice for the priests, of course, because it gave them an extra source of income. I think myself that first cousins shouldn't marry, but when a woman gets under a man's skin, it's no good trying to reason with him.

Something which had to be done in secret during Holy Week was playing dominoes or cards. On Easter Saturday, when the time of penance ended, people played in the door ways, but the rest of the time they had to keep hidden. Skittles were so strictly forbidden, they weren't even played secretly. There were two or three skittle alleys in Remedios which were never used. They held raffles with cards. You bought two cards and either wrote your name on them or marked the backs. The person who distributed the cards collected the money. Someone would take a knife, spike the winning card and hold it up for everyone to see. If it was number seven, whoever had that number won all the money. It's a mystery about number seven; it's like three, and also eight, which is the number of the dead. But playing cards in silence and secrecy was more exciting. The rich whites never did that sort of thing in Holy Week, though; they said there ought to be total mourning for Christ's disappearance. I think they were hypocrites. I know Christ is the son of God and comes from Nature, but this business of his dying seems a bit mysterious to me. As a matter of fact, I have seen him several times myself, but without knowing who it was.

They worked all through Holy Week on the plantations, except on Monday and Tuesday and after ten on Saturday morning, which was the hour of Christ's resurrection. The plantation-owners waited till Christ was risen to crack down on you again. Some people went in for witchcraft after the resurrection. The fiesta in Remedios began at the same time, ten in the morning. Easter Saturday was the most amusing day of the year. A *juá* effigy was burned, like on San Juan's day, a big fat doll strung up on a rope which they beat with sticks and then burned to ashes as a reminder of Judas's betrayal of Jesus. The *juá* represented the enemy of the Christians, the man whom the whites used to say murdered Jesus. He killed Christ during a Jewish war. I was told all about this once, but now it's beginning to get a bit confused in my mind. All I know is that he once existed, and he was Christ's murderer, that I'm sure of.

I never saw a village as riddled with traditions and customs as Remedios. They were quite fanatical. During the fiestas everyone felt obliged to go out and enjoy themselves, but if you didn't act religious during Holy Week you were taken for a monster and said to be in league with the Devil. But of course this was the sort of thing the whites said among themselves, they never talked to the country folk. They went to church and to the fiestas because they were so pious, and the parents made their children pray and take part in the sung masses held in the street. It really made you laugh to see those grown men singing in public—they did it so badly! They used to walk through the streets wearing black, with candles and little black books. The rich women wore tall combs in their hair with little holes in them and looked very pretty.

In those days sons were not entirely independent. It was not till they were twenty-five that they could decide certain things for themselves. Their fathers kept them on a short rein, which is why they spent so much time going to church and praying. This happened in the towns as much as in the country.

There was one fellow who wasn't very friendly towards the Church, called Juan Celorio. He used to get the children together whenever there was a fiesta, and on Sundays too, and play with them and amuse them. He was a Spaniard from Asturias, a store-keeper. As the children arrived he made friends with them by handing out sweets, coffee, bread and butter, and anything else they fancied. He talked to them a lot. He told them they ought to have fun and enjoy themselves instead of going to church. This made the parents so angry they saw red at the mere mention of his name. Celorio was a good man. Whenever the children had a holiday they used to go to see him and have a meal. Then he gave them tins, sheets of corrugated iron, spades, gratings and earthenware jars, filled with wax and decorated with turkey feathers, with a hole at one end to blow through. It created a

tremendous scandal when he organised them into pro-
cessions and marched them through the village, banging,
rattling and blowing all these instruments, while crowds
of people joined in, all looking for a bit of fun. This was
the origin of the famous *parranda*.*

*

I saw other strange things on Easter Saturdays in
Remedios. The place looked like an inferno then, it
was so crowded. Out in the streets you were as likely to
bump into a rich man as a poor one. The street corners
were swarming with people. The village became very
gay, full of lights and flares and fireworks. Then the
puppeteers turned up and started dancing and miming.
I remember them well—there were Spaniards, gypsies
and Cubans. The Cubans weren't much good, they didn't
have the wit or fantasy of the gypsies. The puppeteers
used to perform in parks and halls, but it was much
harder to follow what was going on in the parks because
the crowd was so thick you couldn't see a thing. They
sang and squealed, and the children were thrilled by those
big dolls walking and jerking at the end of a string. There
were other performers who dressed themselves up like
dolls in checked and striped clothes and funny hats. They
used to leap about and give away sweets, eat whatever
you gave them and then lie on the ground on their backs
with a great stone on their bellies, which someone in the
audience was invited to crack open with a giant hammer,
after which the clown jumped to his feet and bowed,

* A local annual festival at Remedios, famous throughout Cuba.

quite unhurt. Everyone imagined that the man's guts would be spilled all over the ground, but that wasn't the case at all. Those people were clever at deceiving, they'd been doing their tricks for so many years they couldn't go wrong. That was how they earned their living. They amused people and got on well with one and all. One of the clowns would eat burning papers and then pull them out of his mouth again, changed to coloured streamers, while the spectators gasped, quite mystified.

The gypsies were the best, both comic and serious. Outside their work they were serious and didn't welcome strangers. They sported the most garish clothes, but the men were rather dirty. They wore jackets and scarves tied round their heads, covering their foreheads, almost always red scarves. The women wore long garish skirts, bracelets on their arms and rings on all their fingers. Their hair was jet-black, waist-length and gleaming. The gypsies came here from their own country. To be honest, I don't remember where it was, but I know it was far away. They spoke Spanish, though. They had no houses, but lived in tents which they made for themselves out of four stout sticks and a piece of thick cloth, and they all slept on the ground wherever they pleased.

In Remedios they camped on vacant lots or in the porches of ruined houses. They rarely stayed long, but spent their lives travelling from one fiesta to the next. Their whole life was like that; on the run and gulping drink. When they liked a place and wanted to stay they moved in the whole tribe, children, animals, everything. Sometimes the Government police had to come and get rid of them. They never protested. They shouldered their sticks and bundles and set off along the road again. They hardly seemed to care even about food, I mean they cooked on the ground. I always liked them. Like the magic-men, they could tell fortunes, but they did it with cards. The women were particularly expert. They almost forced people to listen to them, but they were convincing, because so much travelling had given them a lot of experience. The gypsies had dogs, birds and monkeys trained to dance and hold their paws out for coins. The monkeys were skinny from too little food. The dogs used to dance too, and stand on their hind legs.

I believe there still are gypsies like that in Cuba. It's quite possible, with all their wandering, that they have got lost somewhere in the countryside, in the little villages.

Another Holy Week entertainment was the lotteries, held on Easter Saturday. They raffled scarves, perfumes, rose pomade and sewing-machines—cheap scarves and stinking perfumes. I never wore perfume so as not to catch a chill; there are people who haven't the constitution for it. Nobody ever won the sewing-machines, they were the fools' bait. People went and bought lots of tickets, but I never saw anyone win a sewing-machine, although they spent hours waiting outside the booths hoping for one. It used to enrage me to see them spending all their money without anyone winning. If I had my way I would have put an end to those raffles, if only for the sake of the poor wretches who ended up begging in the streets.

These raffles always took place during Holy Week,

with the support of the priests themselves. Even today raffles are a giant fraud, especially when organised by the Church. About ten years ago I went with all the old veterans on parade to a church near Arroyo Apolo where there are lots of honey-berry bushes. We were invited by the priests. One of them, the one who said mass, tried to win over the old men with the words of Christ and stuff like that. He actually said right in the middle of mass that all communists should be exterminated and that they were the children of Satan. This put me in a rage, because I had been a member of the Popular Socialist Party* for many years on account of its plans and ideals, particularly the welfare of the workers. I never went back to that church, and I never saw the priest again either, but I heard through an old gossip who claimed to be a friend of mine that the priest had organised a fiesta in the church-yard and held a big raffle. When they began handing out the prizes the old men had found themselves with little handkerchiefs and little socks and other rubbish like that. I realised that it was the same old trick and that the raffles were as full of cheating as ever. That's why I never go in for them.

In the old days they used to put on little shows or revues during the Easter Saturday fiestas called 'little salads'. They were very amusing, and you saw the most extraordinary things done in them. All they needed was a few poles and a screen with something painted on it as a backdrop. Quite often it didn't have anything painted on

---

* The name of Cuba's Communist Party until the reorganisation of the Revolution.

it at all. Then the actors appeared and started clowning around, acting like monkeys, singing, making up stories and jokes and riddles, and telling people's fortunes—anything which came into their heads, in fact. It was another trick to get your money out of you. When the shows were put on in a hall everyone had to pay to enter, and whites and blacks alike used to go.

The Cubans have always liked these sort of shows. I went to the theatre once in Havana, and I'm sure what I saw there was a revue; it was a sort of comedy between a white man and a black man. I must say I don't see what's so funny about that, however they dress it up.

Remedios was a great place for old traditions, the things they did there had been going on for years and years. like on Corpus Christi day, when the Negroes came out of their clubs dressed as devils, with bright colours daubed on their clothes, hoods covering their heads and bells round their waists. They frightened the children. But though they came out of the Congolese clubs, they weren't *náñigos*, because there was no *náñiguismo* in Remedios. They were devils of the Congolese religion.

The Negroes in Remedios had two clubs: a recreation centre on the corner of Brigadier Gonzalez Street, and one for religious rites. During Holy Week the recreation club had an all-Negro dance band. *Danzones* were very popular in those days, and Negroes danced them in the streets as well as in the halls. The band didn't only play for Negroes. Sometimes they went along to the Tertulia, the whites' club, and played there for a bit. The musicians were well paid. I never danced to bands myself; my recreation was women. As soon as I got to the village I started sniffing around. Then I cast my line, and I always came up with a good catch.

People in Remedios, as in all the other nearby villages, breakfasted early, and the table was cleared by half-past six or seven. The poor people breakfasted even earlier, especially the country folk, on coffee and sweet potato— delicious sweet potato cooked the African way, in hot cinders. They had lunch at eleven-thirty, and a well-off household always had bread, butter and wine. People didn't drink water then, it was wine, wine, wine.

Dinner was at eight-thirty or nine, the big meal of the day. In the villages people went to bed at midnight, but the country people were fast asleep by eight or nine o'clock. The young gentlemen might rise at ten, but a peasant who had to sweat for his living would be up at five. People drank a lot of coffee, and every household had its big black coffee-pots and roasted its own beans, and if they didn't have a coffee-mill they used a pestle and mortar. I prefer the pestle and mortar myself, because it preserves the aroma, but perhaps that's my imagination. Before there were so many coffee plantations, coffee was sold in apothecary shops and later by street-vendors. It became very profitable. I knew people who did nothing else but sell unroasted coffee-beans.

Agualoja was a very popular drink in Remedios. It was made from water, honey, sugar and vanilla, and sold by special vendors in the street. It smelled beautiful. I drank gallons. The old Lucumi women made the best

agualoja, without skimping or anything. The old Congolese women made it, too.

Whatever an African made was made well, from a
recipe from his own country. My favourite was fritters,
which aren't sold in the streets any more. People don't
appreciate that sort of thing nowadays; they make their
own fritters without salt or lard, and it doesn't taste of
anything at all. You should have seen the trouble they took
making fritters in the old days, especially the old women.
They sold them in the streets on wooden trestles or big
baskets which they carried on their heads. 'Mother
Petrona, Mother Domingo, come here,' you would call
to an old Lucumi woman, and she would bustle over,
very clean and neat in her lawn or cotton dress, and say,
'Five cents, son.' For five or ten cents you could stuff
yourself with fritters of okra, chick peas, *malanga*,
dozens of things. They called these 'snacks'. There were
more vendors on fiesta days than any others, but if you
just wanted fritters, there was always an old woman on
the corner with her cooking-pot ready.

Punch was sold in the streets and in the taverns, but on
fiesta days at least it was easier to get in the streets. I
shall never forget that punch. It didn't have orange juice,
rum, or anything like that, nothing but egg-yolk, sugar
and brandy. You put the ingredients into an earthenware
bowl or a big tin, and beat the mixture up with a wooden
spatula shaped like a pineapple, which you twirled in
both hands. When it was thoroughly mixed you drank
it. The whites of egg weren't added because they curdled
it. It was sold at five cents a glass. Dead cheap! Punch was

very popular at christenings. The Africans always had some of it around to make everyone cheerful, though christenings always were cheerful events in those days— they seemed to turn into parties of their own accord.

The African custom was to baptise children forty days after birth. As the day drew near the godparents began collecting as many half-dollars as they could lay hands on, for they were expected to bring money to the christening. They changed all their coins—doubloons, centenes and so on—for half-dollars, and when they had a big pile of them they took green and red ribbons and threaded all the half-dollars, which had a hole in the centre, on to them. This job was given to the little girls. On the day of the christening the godparents would turn up wreathed in smiles with their pockets full of coins. After the christening and the refreshments, the grown-ups went out into the patio and called to the children, who all came running out. As soon as they were all there the god-parents threw the string of half-dollars into the air, and the kids went mad trying to catch them. This was another of the funny customs of that time, and it was always done in Remedios. That's where the expression 'Half a dollar, godfather' comes from. I was godfather twice, but I don't remember a thing about my godchildren. Everything gets mixed up; some remember other people, and some don't; that's life. There's nothing to be done about it. Ingratitude exists, and that's all there is to it.

*

The most moving sight there is is to see men behaving

in a brotherly way towards each other. This is more common in the countryside than in towns. There are too many worthless people in the city and in the villages, rich slobs who think they're the lords of creation and wouldn't lift a finger to help a living soul. But it's different in the countryside. Everyone there has to live on close terms with everyone else, like a family. There must be happiness.

People were always helping each other in the Las Villas district. Neighbours treated each other like brothers. If a man needed help moving or sowing or burying a relative, he had it at once. A palm-thatched house, for instance, could be put up in two days if everyone got together on the job. They would put a roof on a house for you in a couple of hours, or they might help you with the ploughing. Each neighbour would bring his team of oxen along, then they broke up the soil, first in single furrows and then double-yoked. This made the ground more fertile. The same happened during the sowing; everyone joined in so that the poor man whose fields they were shouldn't get too tired and give up. Knowing that a new neighbour couldn't cope with all the work on his own to begin with, the other smallholders would give him some of their seeds. After the sowing there was the weeding to be done, and so they all lent a hand earthing up to keep the soil soft and fertile. Hard soil doesn't bear, it needs to be turned up.

All this was done as a sign of friendship. There was one trick, a practical joke, which was a bit crude perhaps but amused the country people. One man would start eyeing another man's pigs—all the pigs were branded on the ear with their owner's mark. Well now, if he succeeded in making off with one of the other fellow's animals, he would kill it and give a big fiesta to which all his friends were invited. The roast pig would be placed on a wooden platter on the table, with wild flowers in its mouth and the branded ear well in view. At that point the pig's real owner would realise what a foolish figure he cut, because everybody there was eating his property. This was a joke, though, and you weren't expected to lose your temper. In fact, the owner was expected to be the happiest person there.

I see all this as proof of friendship. People don't behave like that nowadays. Everywhere you look now there is envy and jealousy. That's why I like a solitary life. I don't meddle with other people, so they won't meddle with me. I never went about in a gang even in the old days; I was always on my own. Sometimes a woman would attach herself to me, and I let her, but this idea of sticking to some people for life doesn't agree with me. Being so old now, I have no enemies, and if I had they wouldn't even speak to me for fear of getting into a fight.

*

I knew lots of people in Remedios. I spent my whole time there in the early part of the Nineties. I could get to the village from Ariosa in a twinkling. I knew the customs and the people, and I knew what they were thinking when they looked at you. The rich people were the ones who paid the least attention to gossip; they passed their time with music and dancing, and with their money too, of course.

The village ladies used to play the harp in their drawing-rooms with the windows wide open so everyone could see them. Later the piano arrived, but first it was the harp. I didn't much care for harp music myself, and I always thought it rude to stare into people's houses, although it was the custom. I preferred drums and dance music, the sort the village band used to play. Still, because the harp was a novelty to the Negroes they all used to stop at the windows and stare and stare. The fact is, all those rich families, the Rojas, the Manuelillos and the Carillos, kept pretty much to themselves, and their lives revolved round business, parties and money. They didn't care for gossip. The poor people did, but then they were thrown together more and they were more . . . well, the rich are rich, and the poor are poor.

All this I saw in Remedios. Many Negroes didn't go to the fiestas because they were old or held strictly to the tribal ways, but I used to take a turn round the place for the sake of the girls. Such beauties! Then, at night, I'd take the road back with my machete at my waist in case anyone tried to jump out at me along the way. If it hadn't rained I got to the plantation quickly. If I got too tired along the road I'd drop off to sleep in the cane-fields till my legs felt strong enough to carry on. The cane is cool at dawn.

The other day I suddenly felt like talking about it all, and I got together with some old men and told them what I had seen there. I prefer the old men to the young ones,

I always have, perhaps because I am old now myself . . . but no, before, when I was young, I felt the same. In those days they used to listen to my stories about the fiestas, the *juá*, the food and drink, and the various games and competitions. They would ask me if people behaved decently and respectably, and I was too ashamed to tell them some of the dirty things that went on. I kept my mouth shut. How could you tell old men like that that you were quite capable of having a Negress in the bushes? But just as they listened to you, you had to listen to them, with eyes and ears. They were honest always. They would say to you quite calmly, 'Boy, you not listen, you not attending, you get off home!' and you had to leave with your face burning. Although they didn't talk much, they liked you to pay attention when they did. They talked about the land, Africa, animals and apparitions. They didn't go in for gossip and quarrels, and anyone who lied to them was severely punished. You had to be quiet and respectful to get along with the elders. A boy once made fun of one elder, and he said, 'Listen, when the sun sets, you'll be on your way too.' And so it was, just as happened under slavery; he collected earth the boy had walked on and put it into a pot. That's how the elders rid themselves of people who mocked them. Those old men were amazing. They even knew where the gnat lays its eggs. If you went to them they could untangle anything, for money or even for nothing. When you asked them to do something, they said, 'You go do this magic, and when you solve problem come to me and pay.' You had to do what they said. There was always twenty-five cents to pay before the consultation; this was apart from the other payment, which was bigger. Anyone who didn't pay the larger payment, which was secret, was in bad trouble—he would get stabbed a few days later, or lose his woman or his job . . . something always happened to him. You couldn't play about with those elders from the old country. Nowadays a young priest of the Stick Cult is less exacting; the old Negroes, however, had different ways, they were more serious, more severe.

*

What the old men enjoyed most was telling jokes and stories. They told stories all the time, morning, noon and night, they were at it constantly. There were so many stories that it was often difficult to keep track of them, you got so muddled up. I always pretended to be listening, but to be honest, by the end it was all whirling round in my head. There were three or four African elders at Ariosa. There was a difference between the Africans and the Creoles. The various Africans understood each other, but the Creoles hardly ever understood the Africans. They used to listen to them singing, but they didn't understand them. I got on all right with them because I spent my whole life listening to them. They were fond of me, too.

I still remember Ma Lucia. I first met her outside Ariosa, I don't recall whether it was at Remedios or Zulueta, but in any case I met her again long afterwards at Santa Clara, when I went there to a fiesta. I got on well with Ma Lucia. She was a black-skinned Negress, rather tall, a Lucumi by birth. After I got to know her she devoted most of her time to *santería*. She had a big collection of godchildren, being so well-known. Ma Lucia was a great story-teller. She spent hours ironing her clothes, her white costume and cambric blouse, out of vanity, and she wore her hair in a piled-up style which you never see nowadays. She said it was African. She made sweets and *amalá** which she sold in the streets and in the plantation town when she did the rounds, and she made a lot of money.

She finally bought herself a house in Santa Clara after the war, which she left to a daughter. One day she called me and said, 'You're a good, quiet man, I'm going to tell you something,' and she began telling me all sorts of African stories. Unfortunately, almost all the stories and things I hear get muddled in my memory, and I don't know whether I'm talking about an elephant or a mouse. Old age does this to you. There are some things I remember clearly, but old age is old age, and it isn't given you for pleasure.

The point is, Ma Lucia started telling me about African customs which I never saw here, and nor did she either, which is why they were in her memory. She told me that in her country all the men ever did was fell trees, while the women had to clear the ground and bring in the food, and then cook meals for the family, which was very big. She said her own family was bigger than a slave settlement. I suppose this is because in Africa women give birth every year. I once saw a photograph of Africa, and

* Corn-flour with pork.

all the women had swollen bellies and bare tits. I don't recall seeing such a spectacle in Cuba. Certainly it was quite different in the barracoons—the women there wore layers of clothes and covered their breasts. Well, not to wander too far from Ma Lucia, what she said about the elephants was very strange; whenever she saw one of those circuses which went from village to village, with elephants and monkeys, she would say, 'Look, Creole, you don't know what an elephant is! Those aren't elephants you see in the circus, elephants in my country are much higher, high as a palm-tree heart.' I was struck dumb. It really did seem a bit much to me, especially when she went on to say that in her country elephants weighed five or six hundred pounds. We boys couldn't help laughing at that, though we didn't let on to her. A lot of her stories were lies, but some might have been true. Well, let's say I thought they were lies, though the others thought they were the truth. Heaven help anyone who tried to tell one of those old women she was wrong!

I remember the story of the tortoise and the toad; she must have told it to me a hundred times. The tortoise and the toad had this big feud going for years, and the toad used to deceive the tortoise because he was frightened of her and thought she was stronger than him. One day the toad got hold of a big bowl of food and presented it to the tortoise, setting it down right under her nose, almost in her mouth. When the tortoise saw the bowl she took a fancy to it and gobbled it so fast she choked. It never even crossed her mind that the toad had put it there for a reason. She was very simple-minded, and so it was easy to trick her. After that, feeling full and satisfied, she started wandering through the forest in search of the toad, who had hidden himself in a cave. When the toad saw her in the distance, he called out, 'Here I am, tortoise, look.' She looked but couldn't see him, and after a while she got tired and went away till she came across a heap of dry straw and lay down to sleep. The toad seized her while she was asleep and poisoned her by peeing over her, and she didn't even wake up because she had eaten so heavily. The moral of this story is that people shouldn't be greedy, and you should trust no one. An enemy might offer you a meal merely to trick you.

Ma Lucia went on telling me about the toad. She was afraid of toads because, she said, they had a fatal poison in their veins instead of blood. The proof of this is that when you harm one by hitting it with a stick or a stone, it will follow you and poison you through the mouth or the nose, usually the mouth, because nearly everyone sleeps with their mouth open.

She told me that tigers were treacherous animals who climbed trees so as to be able to spring down on to men's backs and kill them. But they would seize women by their parts and force them to do dirty things with them, like the orang-outangs. But the orang-outangs were worse. According to Ma Lucia an orang-outang could tell a woman by her smell and capture her quite easily, so she couldn't even move. All monkeys are like that, like men with tails, but dumb.

Monkeys often fall in love with women. There have

been cases like this in Cuba. I heard of two women of rich families who slept with monkeys, two sisters. One of them came from Santa Clara. I don't remember much about the other one, but she must have had children, because I saw monkeys lording it about in her house. I had to go along there one day, I can't remember why, and there was this monkey sitting in a chair in the door-way. That's why I think that the elders were sometimes speaking the truth—it was just that we had not seen these things for ourselves, so we either disbelieved them or laughed at them. Today, after so many years, I find my-self thinking about all this again, and to tell the truth, I am coming to the conclusion that the African was a wise man in all matters. Some people say they were no better than monkeys off the trees—there's always some bloody white going round saying things like that—but having known them, I think differently. They weren't the least bit like animals. They taught me many things without being able to read or write—customs, which are more important than knowledge: to be polite, not to meddle in other people's affairs, to speak softly, to be respectful and religious, to work hard. They used to say, 'Water falls on the arum plant but it never gets wet,' which was a warning to me not to get involved in arguments. They advised me to listen and take note so as to be able to stick up for myself, but not to talk too much. A person who talks too much ties himself in knots. Lots of people put their foot in it simply because they let their tongues run away with them.

*

Luckily I have always been a man of few words. I haven't forgotten what the elders told me. Far from it! And when I hear people talking about 'muzzled ones' I have to laugh. Muzzled, indeed! People only called the newly arrived Africans that because they had to call them something, and they only spoke their own language. Their speech sounded different, that was all. I never thought of them as 'muzzled'; on the contrary, I respected them. A Congolese or Lucumi Negro knew more medicine than most doctors, than Chinese doctors, even! They could even tell when a person was about to die. The word 'muzzled' is quite wrong. Not that you hear it very often now, because almost all the African-born Negroes have died, and if there are any left they would have to be twenty times older than me.

All the Negroes were different physically, they had different noses or lips. Some were blacker than the others, or reddish-skinned like the Mandingas, or orangey like the Musongos. You could tell what country they came from a long way off. The Congolese, for instance, were short. There were cases of tall Congolese, but they were rare; the true Congolese were small and stocky, and their women were the same. The Lucumis came in all sizes, some of them almost as tall as the Mandingas, who were the tallest of all. I can't explain this. It certainly is a mystery. Why should some men be taller than others? God knows.

The Lucumis were hard-working, they would take on any kind of job. They even fought well in Carlos Manuel's war. In spite of having no military training, they joined

up and fought like lions. But then, when the war ended,
they had to go back to work, back to being slaves. That
was why they were more cynical about the next war.
But they fought as well as anyone else. I never saw a
Lucumi run away or heard one boasting about his
courage. Other Africans used to say that war was stupid
and settled nothing, and this was because of their
disillusionment. Yet most of them took part in the War
of Independence. I know myself that war destroys men's
trust, your brothers die beside you, and there is nothing
you can do about it. Then along come the smart guys
and grab all the good jobs. Nevertheless, one should fight;
a man who acts like a coward and creeps into a corner
loses his dignity for ever. Those old men volunteered for
the War of Independence with memories of the other war
still fresh in their minds, and they acquitted themselves
well, but without the old enthusiasm. They had lost some
of that, though they had lost none of their strength or
courage. Besides, Heaven alone knew what they were
letting themselves in for!

The cause was a great one, but the new war brought
a lot of confusion. You heard rumours that Spain was
losing and that Cuba was going to be free. But the plain
truth of the matter is that anyone who took part in it was
staking the last card in the pack. That's why you can't
criticise the elders for not being brave. Not only were
they brave, but they were more dependable than the
Creoles. Everyone knows there were Creole guerrillas,
but you would never have got one of those elders to be
a guerrilla. They fought with Carlos Manuel and gave an

example of patriotism. I won't say they knew exactly what they were fighting for, but they went all the same. When things are bad there's no time for wavering, what you have to do is get in there and fight. The Cuban of that time, in '68, wasn't trained to fight. He had the courage in his heart but nothing in his hands. It was harder to find a weapon then than a needle in a haystack, but that didn't stop them making daggers out of indigo-wood. They used these against an enemy supplied with firearms. It was usually the Congolese who made them. Anyone they struck with them went quite stiff. I think they must have had some magic on the point. If a Spaniard saw a Negro with one of those daggers he took to his heels. They also used muskets in the Ten Years' War.

There were enough weapons for us in the War of Independence. The fighting was on more equal terms, and that's why we won. We had muskets, heavy-calibre guns, carbines and some rifles. The heavy calibres were scarcely used, because ammunition was hard to get. Winchester rifles were very popular, and so were blunder-busses, which were the bandits' favourite weapons. The African-born Negroes, like the Creoles, learned to use all these weapons and fought like devils. They were better equipped in this war.

Whenever I see one of those Negro elders in my mind, I see him fighting. They didn't talk about what they were fighting for, or why, they just went and did it. It was in defence of their lives, of course. If you asked them how they felt, they said, 'Free Cuba, I'm a liberator.' None of them wanted to continue under Spanish rule. You can

swear on your mother's grave that's true. None of them
wanted to be shackled again, or eating jerked beef, or
cutting cane at dawn. So they took up arms. And they
didn't want to stay behind, because if one of the Negro
elders was left behind he was very lonely and died of a
broken heart. Those African-born Negroes were good
men, full of jokes and stories. You couldn't leave them
shut up in a barracoon with no one to talk to!

A lot of them joined the battalions because their sons
or nephews had. They put themselves at the command of
the officers, who were Creoles. They did early morning
guard duty, kept watch, cooked, washed, cleaned the
fire-arms—all these duties fell to them. Not one of these
'muzzled ones' became an officer in the war. There were
three or four of them in the platoon I was in, led by
Higinio Esquerra. One was called James, another
Santiago; both Congolese. One of them, I think it was
the older one, was always saying, 'We not frightened
war. We accustomed. In Africa we much fighting.' Over
there they had warlike tribes who fought against each
other, women as well as men, and killed each other in
these disputes. It was like what happened here in the
districts of Havana—Jesús María, Belén, Manglar—
when the *náñigos* set about each other in the African way.
It was just the same. And you can't say it's because they
were savages, because the whites who went in for
náñiguismo did the same.

If the Africans didn't know exactly what they were
fighting for, neither did the Cubans, that is, the majority
of them. What happened is that there was a revolution,

[169]

a big rebellion, in which everyone got involved, even the smartest. People shouted, 'Free Cuba! Down with Spain!' and, 'Long live the King!' I don't know! It was crazy. The only way out was war.

At first no one explained the revolution, you joined in because you wanted to. I never thought of the future. I just shouted, 'Free Cuba!' The leaders began rounding people up and trying to explain it all to them, they spoke to all the battalions. First they said they were proud to be Cubans, and that the *Grito de Baire* had united us all. They urged us to fight, they were certain we would win. A hell of a lot of people thought it was going to be some sort of carnival to win honours in! When they came up against bullets they ran away and betrayed their comrades. There were plenty like that, but also ones who stood firm. One thing which raised everyone's spirits was Maceo's speech at Mal Tiempo. He said, 'This is a War of Independence. Every soldier who gets through it will be paid thirty pesos.'

That was all I heard, and it was true, every word. After the war they paid me nine hundred and eighty-two pesos. Everything Maceo said was true. He was the greatest man of that war. He said no one would come off the loser because we would come out of it free, and that's how it was. At least I didn't lose anything myself, not even my health. I got a bullet wound in one leg, and when I lift up my trouser-leg I still see a black mark. But there were some who never left the forest, they went from horseback to below ground.

The fact is, the war was necessary. The dead would

have died anyway, and this way they were dying for a purpose. I stayed alive by chance, it seems my time hadn't yet come. The gods send different tasks to each of us. I talk about all this now and I can laugh about it, but in the thick of the fighting, with dead bodies all over the place, bullets and cannon balls and all hell let loose, it was different. The war was needed. It was wrong that so many jobs and privileges should fall into Spanish hands, or that women should have to sleep with Spaniards to get work. None of this was right. You never saw a Negro lawyer, because they said Negroes weren't good for anything except the forest. You never saw a Negro schoolmaster. It was all kept for white Spaniards, even the white Creoles were pushed aside. I saw this happen. A watchman with nothing to do except walk up and down, call the hour and put out the lights had to be a Spaniard. It was the same everywhere. There was no freedom. I realised this when the leaders explained it all to us. This was why we had to go to war.

PART III

THE WAR OF
INDEPENDENCE

Life as a Revolutionary Fighter

I JOINED in the war on the third or fourth of December, 1895. I was at Ariosa still, but keeping informed of everything. One day I got together with some friends, the oldest people on the plantation, and I told them we ought to pluck up courage and join in properly. The first person to follow my example was Juan Fabregas, a bold, resolute Negro. I hardly had to tell him anything; he guessed what I was planning to do. We left the plantation in the evening and walked till we got to a farm, where we took the first horses we came across, tethered to a tree. This wasn't stealing, because I took care to ask the farmer for them properly. 'Please be so kind as to give me a saddle,' which he did, and I put it straight on the horse with the reins and spurs. I had everything I needed to go to war. I had no fire-arms, but a machete was enough for those days. I rode hard along the highway, almost as far as Camagüey.

When I came across the rebel forces I shouted to them, and they turned and saw me and the men with me. From that day onwards I gave myself wholly to the war. I felt a bit strange at first, half bewildered. Everything was in a hell of a mess. The platoons hadn't been drawn up yet, or any officers appointed, but even under these conditions there was discipline. We were never short of bloody fools and bandits, but it was the same in the war of '68, so they tell me.

I came down from Camagüey with the rest of the men as far as Las Villas. Things were different by then, because you feel more confident when you are united. I was making friends with everyone so as not to start on the wrong foot, and by the time we got to Mal Tiempo everyone knew me, at least by sight. Fabregas was better at making friends than I was, and he won the troops over in no time at all, telling stories and teasing them all like mad. I didn't get involved in any fighting before Mal Tiempo, that was my first taste of war. It was also the first time the Spaniards had ever taken punishment in Cuba. Our leaders knew what was going to happen long before we got there and warned us so that we should be prepared. It all happened just as they said it would. The devil was in us all by the time we got to Mal Tiempo. Our weapon was the machete, and our leaders told us, 'As soon as you arrive, raise your machetes.'

Maceo directed the battle, he was in command from the outset. Máximo Gómez helped him, and between them both they won the day. Máximo Gómez was courageous, but secretive. His head was full of schemes. I never trusted him. The proof came later, proof that he was disloyal to Cuba, but that's flour from another sack.

We had to stick together at Mal Tiempo, and as soon

as one man rolled back his sleeves and raised his machete, the rest had to follow. Mal Tiempo lasted about half an hour, but it left enough dead to fill hell. More Spaniards fell there than in all the later battles. The fighting began in the morning on a smooth, open field; a plain. A man accustomed to hill fighting went through some bad moments at first. Mal Tiempo was a little village surrounded by streams and cane-fields and pineapple fences. After the slaughter was over, we saw rows of Spaniards' heads lying among the pineapples. It was one of the most shocking things I have ever seen.

When we got to Mal Tiempo, Maceo ordered us to attack head on. The Spaniards went cold with fear when they saw us. They thought we were armed with blunder-busses and Mausers, but all we had were lengths of guava-tree which we had cut in the forest and carried under our arms to frighten them with. They went crazy when they saw us and flung themselves on us, but their attack was over in the twinkling of an eye. In a moment we were cutting off heads, really slicing them off. The Spaniards were shit scared of machetes, though they didn't mind rifles. I used to raise my machete a long way off and shout, 'I'll have your head now, you bastard!' and then my little toy soldier would turn tail and fly. Not having criminal instincts, I used to let him go. In spite of that, I had to cut a few heads off, especially if I saw one of them about to rush me. A few of them were brave, the minority, and these had to be wiped out. Generally I asked for their Mausers. I said, 'Hands up.' They answered, 'Listen, friend, if it's the Mauser you want, take it!' They threw a lot of Mausers at me, they were a pack of cowards.

Others gave up because they were very green and young. The conscripts, for instance, were only sixteen or seventeen, fresh out from Spain. Most of them had never fought before. When they got into a serious fix they would drop everything, even their pants. I came across lots of these boys at Mal Tiempo, and afterwards as well. I suppose they sent them over because there were too many of them in Spain.

The battalion of Canary Islanders was the bravest one fighting at Mal Tiempo. They were well equipped, but nearly all of them fell because of this same fear of the machete. They disobeyed their officers, flinging themselves down on the ground, dropping their guns and even hiding behind trees. But in spite of this weakness they were the ones who put up the stiffest resistance. They used a very clever tactic, but once we broke their formation they cracked up completely. They formed what are called squares, dug themselves into holes from which they fired kneeling with bayonets presented. Sometimes the trick worked, sometimes not.

Mal Tiempo was the overthrow of this technique. The first moments were difficult for us, but after that, with their squares all in confusion, they had no choice but to fire at random. They bayoneted our horses and blasted the riders with their guns. They were like madmen, blundering about, and the carnage was terrible. Fear was the greatest enemy.

The truth is, we Cubans acquitted ourselves well. I

saw a lot of men charging right through the bullets, they were like cotton-balls to us; what mattered was the ideals, the things we were fighting for, like Maceo said, and Máximo Gómez too, though he never carried out any of them. Mal Tiempo really stirred up the Cubans and gave them new heart.

They tried to kill me at Mal Tiempo. A little fellow from Galicia saw me from a distance and aimed, but I got hold of him by the collar and spared his life. He was killed a few minutes later, but all I did was take away his ammunition and gun, and maybe his clothes too. But I'm not sure I took his clothes, because our own weren't too bad. This Galician looked at me and said, 'You are a lot of savages.' Then he turned and ran, and they killed him. Of course we seemed like savages to them, because they were such tame people themselves. The trouble was they really didn't know what they were doing, they seemed to think war was a game, and when things got hot they started to run. They began to think of us as animals rather than men. That was how we came to be called *Mambises*, because *mambi* is an African word meaning the child of an ape and a vulture. It was an ugly phrase, but we made use of it when we cut off their heads. This was one of the things they discovered at Mal Tiempo. It got so that instead of *mambis* they had to call us lions, as was clearly shown at Mal Tiempo. It was the biggest slaughter of the war, and it happened like that because it had been predestined. Some things are inevitable. The twists of life are very complicated.

Mal Tiempo was needed to encourage the Cubans and

strengthen the revolution. Anyone who fought there came out of it confident that he could deal with the enemy. Maceo had said so many times on the way there, in the plains. He was certain of winning, or at least, that's the impression he gave. He never wavered or weakened, he was harder than a hardwood tree. Without Maceo, things would have been different. We would have failed.

The Spanish said that he and his brother José were criminals, but this is a lie. He wasn't addicted to killing. He would kill for the cause, but I never heard him say that you should lop people's heads off, which was what other men were saying and doing every day. Of course, some killing was necessary. You can't go to war and stand there with your arms folded, because that's a coward's role.

Maceo behaved like a real man at Mal Tiempo. He was always out in front, and he rode an Arab horse even braver than he was. It never seemed to stumble on anything. After he had broken through the fire of the Spaniards crouched on the ground with bayonets fixed, he came closer to our platoon and I was able to take a closer look at him. The firing was dying down a bit, though you could hear shots from time to time. Maceo was tall, stout, with moustaches, and very talkative. He gave orders which he was the first to carry out. I never saw him strike a common soldier ever. Not once! But any colonel who acted insubordinately would feel the back of his hand in a flash. He said ordinary soldiers weren't responsible for mistakes.

*

Besides Maceo and Gómez there were other very
brave men at Mal Tiempo, Quintin Banderas for one.
He was as black as a lump of coal, but livelier than anyone except Maceo. Quintin had fought in the other war,
the war of '68. He had the spirit for this sort of thing,
perhaps he enjoyed it, he was a belligerent sort of man.
I've been told he joined up to fight for the Negroes, but
people say stupid things. Anyway, it's true the Negroes
supported him. I myself trusted him. I saw him many
times, at Mal Tiempo and afterwards. Because he had
been fighting other engagements on the way he arrived
at Mal Tiempo late and with two mules, two women
and a small handful of men. The Spanish were thrown
into a panic by the mere sight of him. He was always
risking his neck, escaping, and then mocking them and
cutting the heads off the ones who lost their nerve. He
would ask, 'What is your name?' and as the man started to
reply, he'd say, 'It *was*, you mean,' and cut off his head.

Banderas fell out with Máximo Gómez at Mal Tiempo.
I don't know what the cause was, but all Banderas's men
noticed it, and it happened a couple of times more
after that. When Banderas was on his way back from
Mal Tiempo, he had to take part in the battle of Olayita,
near Rodrigo. He lost almost all his men. He put up a
good fight, but things went wrong. There was a strip of
marshy ground there, and all the horses got stuck in it,
and it turned into an immense quagmire. Then someone,
I don't know who, accused him of being on the point of
surrendering to the Spanish, but this was only because
of the popular prejudice against Negroes. It's true, there

were Negro guerrillas and scabs, but there was nothing but good to say of Banderas. Máximo Gómez wanted to place him under the command of Carillo, who wasn't a general or anything like, but Maceo eventually cleared the matter up and Quintin returned to fight with his troops.

I have seen many brave men, but the only man as brave as Banderas was Maceo. Yet Banderas had a bad time under the Republic; they never gave him a proper chance. The bust they made of him was left lying on the quayside for years, although it was the statue of a patriot. That's why the people are still so turbulent; because they lack respect for their real liberators. If you tell people about that bust, they think you must be lying, but I saw it myself. I don't know where it can be now; maybe they set it up again.

I'd put up ten busts of Banderas, one for each battle. He deserves them. He wiped out a whole crowd of Canary Islanders at Mal Tiempo. I should think at least half the Spaniards killed there were brought down by him. Hundreds of them! The whole place was choked with bodies, the ditches, the verges of the fields, everywhere. The *Mambises* filled wagons with corpses to be taken to Cruces. I didn't take part in that operation, I had enough to do with the men who had fallen beside me, hacked about.

*

After the victory we got ready to march on, but with more confidence now. I remember we were still quite disorganised, and there were constant quarrels and disputes about the leadership. The platoons hadn't yet been drawn up, and we were really just drifting along. There was plenty of fighting spirit, but no organisation. Maceo and Gómez were the principal leaders, but they couldn't control everybody under their command. I think the first place we reached was the Las Nieves plantation, where we got weapons and equipment. Then we went straight on to Olayita, where we fought alongside Banderas in the marshy land by the stream. The enemy forces were very well placed there. Our own horses slipped and fell, sod them, which is why the Banderas affair turned out so badly.

Then we reached El Mamey, where there was hard fighting. Our side was united, and though the Spanish put up some resistance we taught them another lesson. Then we headed for other plantations. We were approaching Matanzas by now, still without fixed leadership. We passed through the España and Hatuey plantations and seized a load of arms. Around that time, Máximo Gómez and Cayito Alvarez began to name leaders and create small walking groups for the march. It was a difficult time, not everyone was happy with their commanding officers. No one mutinied, out of decency, but many of the officers were wild, lawless men. I got Tajó, the bandit and highwayman, whom I knew well. I didn't like accepting his orders, but there was no help for it; you can't argue about things in war, you just have to obey. Tajó pitched camp on the El Capitolio hill, a funny little hill between Jicotea, San Diego and Esperanza. The camp was beside a big cotton-tree, with a thicket behind and, below, a smooth, empty space. The camp was not very big, but it was kept well supplied. It was difficult to get to as you had to climb the hill between bushes and clumps of grass, and no Spaniards ever dared make the ascent. Tajó used to sit for hours repeating, 'You won't get any Spanish bastards trying to climb up here.' Then he rolled about, laughing. He was more malicious than all the rest of us put together, and he would have liked to make a big headquarters of this one small camp. Of course we knew all the ways in and out of the camp; one of the easiest was through the farm gates, a gate called the 'Red Gate'. We used it, and so did Tajó's men and women friends.

Tajó was very friendly with one Daniel Fuentes, who was a Cuban and pretended to act as guide to the Spaniards in the region. They had been friends back in peace time. I never liked the man myself, and I kept telling Juan Fabregas so—the man who left Ariosa at the same time as I did. Juan was very calm and never said anything, but I remained suspicious. At first I thought that Tajó was planning to surrender, but then I realised I was wrong and that Daniel was in fact informing Tajó about all the Spanish manoeuvres. This is why we were never found or even fired at.

Whenever a guerrilla band or an enemy column was about to pass, Daniel used to let us know in advance. I still disliked the man, though, because he was a turncoat, on your side one day and on the other the next. But I never dared say anything to Tajó about it, because I knew what was going through his mind, and it always seemed to me that he was up to something wicked, I could see it in his eyes. Whenever I saw him leave the look-out post and everyone was keeping silent, I knew that Daniel Fuentes had been talking again. Tajó would give the order to leave the look-out post, and the whole troop waited in silence as the Spaniards went by in the distance, neat and starched on their Arab horses. It would have been difficult for them to see us in any case, as our camp was immaculately tidy, not even any rubbish about. Everyone slept on the ground. Most soldiers then lived in camps of palm shacks and huts.

Tajó had other spies, including Felipe el Sol, who later worked for Cayito Alvarez and others. Spies disgust me, they are like headless puppets. Felipe el Sol saved our lives more than once, but for all that I never trusted him. His favourite game was strolling through the camp, boasting about not having any duties, but no one paid any attention to him, and I didn't even look at him. I spent long hours telling Fabregas what a swine this man was, too.

We had no casualties during the time I fought under Tajó; there were forty men in the troop when I joined, and the same number when I left. The walking groups were lightly equipped, which is why they gave them that name. They didn't have a fixed position and could move about freely. Everyone was very alert. There wasn't much military discipline, I suppose, or experience of fighting, and we did some silly things. Two or three of us used to break out of camp at night, with Tajó's consent some-times, and make for the nearby farms to steal a good-size

pig weighing from 75 to 100 lbs. The Madrazos farm was
the largest and the best for us, because they went in for
pig-breeding. We set out late, round ten at night, on
horseback, and it was on horseback that we caught the
pigs, which were pretty wild, more like boars. They
weren't raised to be fattened and were left wandering
about loose. We gave chase to the first one we saw, it
was like a game to us, and when it got tired one of us would
give it a great blow in the leg with a machete from horseback. The leg would fly off and the pig stopped running.
Then we fell on it and made it fast by the neck and beat
a hasty retreat. The snag about this method of pig-
catching was that the pig bled and squealed a lot.

We were ambushed one night as a result of those
squeals. They didn't catch us, but we were very frightened. The following night we went straight back to the
same place from sheer bravado, more than four of us
this time. No one saw us, or if they did they lay low and
kept quiet. We kept on going there, and every time we
stole a bit more, but we never heard another shot. I
think they were afraid of us. They saw that a different
lot of us went every day, and this frightened them.

I stayed three months with Tajó, but one day I decided
I had had enough and I left. He went too far, he stole
and sold livestock, in short he was a disaster, a cattle-
thief masquerading as a liberator. There were many
others like him.

The day I'm referring to, José, Tajó's brother, who
fought beside him throughout the war, came up to me
looking a bit odd and said, 'Listen, Esteban, I don't

want you to say anything, just come along and help me bury Cañón.' Cañón was a very brave lad in the group, and when I heard this my blood ran cold. I went up to the first person I saw and said, 'Here, what's this, Cañón is dead?' And he said yes, he was, and not to ask so many questions. Then the swine had the cheek to start to explain, 'Cañón was always stealing, son. A thief like that is no good . . .'

I found Cañón hanging from a tree, and the rope was as thick as my arm. It sounded like a pack of lies to me, I knew Cañón was a decent lad. A couple of days later I found it was all the fault of a woman who used to come and see Cañón every night. Tajó fell in love with her, although he had a woman of his own, and so he killed Cañón. I ran to where Juan was and said, 'Juan, I'm leaving. Cayito is at El Plátano, not far away.' Juan didn't fail me, he followed me to El Plátano and there we placed ourselves under the command of Cayito Alvarez. Three months later I heard that Tajó had surrendered to the Spanish, to the party which wanted home-rule under the Spanish Crown. It was just what you would expect of him. He was so fickle that after surrendering he escaped and went back to the liberating army. Holy Moses, what a twister!

The war was fought with men like that. For better or worse, however, fought it was. They reduced Tajó from the rank of captain to common soldier, but it hardly seemed to affect him; there isn't much difference between a plain soldier and a captain. They brought a mass of charges against him. They really made big trouble for him!

After the war I saw him in El Sapo, a little farm where he lived near La Esperanza. He must have been about sixty then. I greeted him, and he greeted me and asked me in. He didn't say anything about my deserting him. He knew quite well that I knew where his weak spots were. He gave me a fighting-cock, which I later sold.

Tajó must be dead now. Hell is too good for a man like that, but that's where he must be. A man who kept sleeping with his own daughters and didn't even let them marry, and who made such a mess of things in the war must be in hell.

Things were not much better with Cayito. I suspected this from the first, and as the days went by my suspicions were confirmed. Cayito was a colonel, a brave, ruthless man. He kept his whole regiment under very harsh discipline, and I don't think this was a good thing—sometimes a gentle hand on the reins is necessary. These men who think they are God Almighty always come a cropper, and that is what happened to Cayito. He was a bastard, I knew that as soon as I laid eyes on him. A sergeant called Felix went up to him and said, 'Colonel, there are some of Tajó's men here.' Cayito looked us up and down, and we signed on and said nothing. But I noticed everything, and I heard Cayito calmly saying, 'Just what I expected of Tajó. I've been expecting him to crack for a long time now. The man's a fraud.'

Those remarks summed him up; cold, a man who sees a crime and makes no protest. Oh well, it was just my bad luck—out of the frying-pan into the fire, going from one thief and murderer to another. Anyone who fought

with Cayito will bear me out. He'd have your head off for
the slightest disobedience. If he had had his way, this
island would be one big cemetery.

There was no stepping out of line in that regiment.
All Cayito had to do was give a soldier a certain look as
he walked past him, and the man would be left trembling
for hours. There was hardly any difference between
Cayito and Tajó, they were two murderous villains
who sneaked into the war. They must have known each
other well. Certainly Cayito was always talking about
Tajó—only to say bad things about him, of course.

All the same, when all's said and done, Cayito was the
quieter of the two. Tajó was a bolder adventurer. Cayito
liked strategy where Tajó liked violence. I know this
because I fought with both of them. I did more fighting
under Cayito, or, to be exact, more hand-to-hand fighting.
But to tell the truth, things weren't too tough with either
of them. Mal Tiempo was my worst experience of the
war, the most tragic one. Of all our encounters with the
Spanish troops only two stand out in my mind, because
there was shooting and danger, and we just managed to
save our skins. To another liberating army they might
have seemed child's play. Still, you tend to remember
times when your life hangs by a thread.

Cayito himself directed one of these encounters, and
his command was firm but arrogant. Whenever danger
came too close he used to finger and twirl his moustache.
This was a little habit of his, the sign of a man of character.

He never once left the camp, and this led a few people
who didn't know him to call him a coward. There are

people who speak ill of the man today, but anyone who attacks his courage is barking up the wrong tree. People say he was small, plump and dark, when he was tall, thin and blond, so it's unwise to take what they say too seriously. They just invent stories, and it's a bad thing. There are a lot of things I could say about him, that he was a murderer and a bandit, for instance, but I wouldn't ever accuse him of cowardice. There were not many men like him in a crisis. He used to defeat the Spanish by using bombs. He concealed various bombs along the path into the camp, and he would blow them up whenever an enemy guerilla band came near. The explosions always frightened the soldiers off, and their horses would vanish in a cloud of dust. I remember Cayito used those bombs in the first engagement I fought under him. They had fuses yards long. The look-out gave the word that someone was approaching by firing a shot in the air. Then the man in charge of the bombs jumped up, grabbed the plunger, gave it a push, and a few seconds later it looked as if the world was coming to an end. There were men screaming, horses careering about all mutilated, legs dangling from trees, and bits of heads rolling about the place, to appear all dried up a few days later, along with a terrible stench, because unburied bodies give off a dreadful smell after a while. The Spaniards were very frightened of the bombs, and Cayito won most of his victories in the war with them.

The first fight was soon over with. We killed off a gang of conscripts who had come up to nose around. But the second was trickier, and we had to play all our cards that time. There was a convoy for Manicaragua coming up from some place I can't remember, heavily laden with supplies, and it had to pass right through the middle of us, over the El Plátano plantation. A spy warned us that they were coming, and Cayito summoned his men and told them, 'Now we will all have to fight like lions.' No one was frightened; on the contrary, they were all raring for action. Cayito went on giving orders. He drew up a long firing line and then went to inspect the infantry, after which he strolled out through the camp, laughing. A short while later we heard shouts. Cayito was shouting like a savage. The convoy was trapped, and we took the soldiers prisoner and seized their arms and food: rice, butter, pork, ham, the lot. We ate like kings for days and days, not just the men but the women too, the officers' women. Cayito had his woman there. Her name was María, and she lived in quite a decent hut. I often went to take her her meals.

The Spanish prisoners remained there under guard. No one spoke to them. Some of the men wanted to kill them, but there was some regulation or other forbidding one to kill prisoners of war. Cayito didn't agree with this, he would have liked to liquidate them all on the spot. He shouted at them, 'You buggers deserve to die!' They kept pretty quiet at this, because they were young soldiers and frightened of us. We didn't give them anything to eat, but after two or three days we set them free and sent them off to the village.

There were no more encounters at El Plátano; it seems as though Cayito must have frightened the Spanish

away. He was a man of spirit, with more guts than anyone in his regiment. No one ever rebelled against his
authority. There can't have been many people who didn't
know about the horrible things he used to do. The village
of Cruces knew that he killed his own soldiers. He even
murdered his own father-in-law so that he could carry
off his wife. There are people today who seem to think
that's funny, but to me it's a crime.

*

Once Cayito buried some money at El Plátano. He had
a passion for hiding money, crocks of gold. No one knows
where he hid it, and there is no way of finding out. What
happened is that Cayito took his adjutant with him to
bury the money and then killed him with his own hands.
Some say he buried him right there. I don't know. But
a few days later he was walking about looking gloomy
and thoughtful. They told me it was because he believed
one of his men had seen where he buried the money. The
camp was uneasy for several days. I found myself thinking, 'Well, if he gets it into his mind that it was me who
saw him burying the money and the adjutant, he'll most
likely throw me into the hole as well.'

But a few days later things calmed down. A blond
mulatto got given the military stocks around that time,
but nothing to do with the money. The stocks were a
hellish punishment, and Cayito inflicted them on anyone who didn't fall in with his ideas.

They gave it to me once. It was an officer I had disobeyed; I had left the look-out post without telling him.

He called me and said, 'Listen, Esteban, you are un-disciplined.' I answered back because I wasn't going to listen in silence, and to be quite honest I can't remember what I said. They grabbed me on the spot. The big-mouth called a couple of men who tied my hands with a cord, or I would have escaped. Then they tied a carbine between my legs so that I couldn't move them and left me like that for a whole day. It was so painful I was seeing stars, but thinking back, I could have come off a lot worse. They used to call a man who left the look-out a deserter and a traitor, and frequently he was hanged. I got away with my life, but I still find myself thinking uncompli-mentary things about that man's mother from time to time.

After that he and I were always spying on each other. He was down on me the whole time, because he saw that I was rebellious. Whenever he could he kept me back in the camp, knowing that what I liked was going out at night to steal pigs and livestock. I was handy at those operations, and even Cayito knew that.

But this officer was always keeping me in to annoy me, and it did annoy me because when I couldn't get out I felt I was in prison. I think that stealing animals was what I did most of during the war. We had to do it because there was no way of growing crops, and we had to eat somehow or other. The people who carried out these exploits were highly thought of. Cayito called me to him one day and said, 'Negro, you bring us food, now join my escort.' I said nothing but I did as I was told, and found myself carrying out new commands, rather clearer than the old ones. I used to go out every night and bring back calves and pigs, splendid ones. Some of them were wild, some tame. Someone else always went with me because one man on his own couldn't cope with a job like that.

There were some places where you could actually grow crops, but Las Villas wasn't one of them. Camagüey was a quiet place, for instance, with scarcely any fighting, and the soldiers sowed crops there and even made gardens. It was full of farms and big houses belonging to rich people, and hardly any Spanish soldiers went near it. It was the province which saw the least fighting. But Las Villas was different. The Spanish there used to burn down the houses of revolutionaries, and a lot of the countryside was held by their guerrilla bands. And this isn't talk, because I saw it with my own eyes.

The most a revolutionary in Las Villas could hope to do was steal livestock and malanga, sweet potatoes, amaranth and purslaine. Mango flour made by cooking up the mango flesh without the stones and adding lemon juice and chili powder to it was our wartime food. And of course a lot of *agua de curujey** was drunk. People were always thirsty. You don't feel hungry after a while in a war, but you do feel thirsty.

The horses grew skinny and old before their time. You couldn't give them *agua de curujey*. The only solution was to take them to a brook somewhere. Water was one of our chief problems, and this was why the commanders

---

* Fluid secreted by a large growth on certain resinous trees. Castro's followers also drank it in the mountains.

always tried to pitch camp near a river. I know of cases
where the guards left their posts and ran away to look
for water. When they got back they were put in the
stocks. I never did this, but I often felt like it.

*

There were all sorts of men in the troop, good and bad.
I didn't have many friends. Juan and Santiago were my
closest friends because they had both come from Ariosa
with me, although I didn't like Santiago all that much, he
was too bloodthirsty and stupid. He always minded his
manners with me, but he hid things from me, and I
only found out about a lot of his tricks through his
brother. Santiago was really thick, he used to shout
'Free Cuba!' till he was hoarse. One day he got tired of
Cayito and ran away without a word to his brother or
me. Soon afterwards we heard he'd been dumb enough to
give himself up to the Spaniards at Jicotea. They immediately accused him of having murdered a Galician
who had been out collecting herbs in the forest. This
took him so much by surprise that he couldn't think of
anything to say in self-defence, and they sentenced him
to death. They shot him through the head and hanged
him in the doorway of a palm-bark house which they then
set fire to. This served as a warning to lots of little Cuban
fellows who couldn't make up their minds where their
sympathies lay. I have never forgotten that incident,
and the only thing it makes me feel is rage. There were
lots of men like Santiago, which meant you couldn't
even trust your friends. If they had forced him to talk

he would certainly have told them everything, but they didn't even give him the chance.

The best thing in war is not to trust people, and the same is true in peace, though it's more essential in wartime. You should never trust anyone. This isn't sad, because it's true. There are good men and bad ones, and the hard thing is to tell one from the other. I have often been mistaken during my life.

*

Cayito Alvarez wouldn't trust even a tomato's mother, and he was quite right. He had many enemies, almost all the men hated him deep down. They saw what he did, his stealing and killing, and they couldn't help but hate him. There were lots of good men in that war who hated in silence, the strongest hate there is.

I watched him closely while I was fighting for him. He was not the kind of man to rejoice when new men joined the troop. If someone came along to join up, he would call him over and talk to him, and sometimes he used to send him off to join another outfit. He did this when he saw a man couldn't be trusted, and by this he meant trusted to keep quiet about his crimes and misdeeds. I can say all this openly now, but then I was almost a prisoner.

Cayito went as far as to turn down entire groups of volunteers. It sometimes happened that an officer died and his men were left leaderless, in which case they had to go and join some other regiment. This often happened

at El Plátano. Men came and we stopped them, and sometimes they stayed and sometimes they were told to take
themselves off somewhere else. As the group approached
we would call out to them to halt, 'Halt! Leader of
the group, step forward!' One man would come forward
and identify himself, and if the group were large, someone was sent to find the officer in command for the day,
the man authorised by Headquarters to let them pass.
Meanwhile everyone in the camp kept themselves at the
ready, just in case, with their rifles trained on the new
arrivals. As the minutes passed the tension eased, friends
would greet each other, sometimes men would meet
members of their own family, and this was how a new
outfit joined the regiment.

If the leaders agreed, the group would be sent to sign
on, and after that they belonged. A lot of men came to
fight for Cayito that way. I think the same happened in
other places and with other leaders. No one was allowed
to join simply because they felt like it. The war was a very
serious business, and not everyone was loyal. I heard of
some Spaniards who infiltrated a troop at Matanzas by
passing themselves off as *Mambises* and it ended in an
ugly bloodbath. That was why everyone took so many
precautions.

The captains and colonels themselves were always
quarrelling, from hatred, envy or hypocrisy, and this
resulted in many deaths and much bloodshed. Not
everyone who fought in the war had the stomach for it.
When some of them saw a lighted fuse they started to
run and panicked, even the colonels. Maceo's death had a

[197]

bad effect on morale; afterwards several officers surrendered to the Spanish. Surrender to Spain in the middle of
the Cuban forest! It was the lowest, vilest thing a man
could do, it was disgusting!

Well, this is what Cayito himself wanted to do. The
son-of-a-bitch kept his plan very secret, although lots
of people were beginning to have their doubts about him,
including me. But the man was such a ferocious brute
that no one dared say anything in case they found themselves trampled underfoot. I can just imagine some poor
wretch who dared start a rumour to that effect—I really
believe that that swine Cayito would have torn him to
pieces and eaten him mouthful by mouthful. Luckily
no one said anything; the ferment was boiling up under-
neath. Felipe el Sol was the one who denounced the
whole plot. That was typical of him. I wasn't there that
day, but I know he went to Leonardo Fuentes and one
Remigio Pedroso, who belonged to Cayito's bodyguard,
and said, 'The man is planning to surrender. I know this
from a reliable source.' They were both tough, good
revolutionaries, and they reacted well. They let a few
trustworthy men into the secret. Everyone was stunned
by the news, but keyed for action. They waited a few
days for Felipe el Sol to return, which he did a week
later with the news that the Spanish troops were coming
the following morning to meet Cayito and a few of his
followers. At that the rest of us got together and decided
that Remigio should kill Cayito at an agreed moment.
Just then Remigio appeared all wide-eyed to tell us,
'Cayito took me aside just now and ordered me to tell

you all that he was planning to surrender. I said nothing, and promised to carry out his order. He also told me that the Spanish are going to give him 15,000 pesos, which he will share out with his men and that he is to receive the rank of colonel in the Spanish army. I congratulated him, and now here I am to carry out whatever orders you give me.' After we had heard this, we decided that it must definitely be Remigio who killed Cayito.

Remigio agreed. The Spanish were to arrive at seven in the morning. Remigio would be waiting, and instead of announcing to the men that Cayito was giving himself up he would take him to a certain mango grove—which must still be there today—and kill him.

The day dawned early. General Duque was approaching in charge of the Spanish column which was to receive Cayito. Other Cuban colonels had already surrendered, and Cayito would not have been alone because Vicente Núñez and Joaquín Macagua had come from their respective regiments to surrender with him. The three of them met a long way off from El Plátano. Cayito's escort was with him, and I, naturally, was one of them. Remigio was ready and waiting. He took Cayito and the other two colonels to the mango grove, and we had them there cold. Some people say that it was Leonardo Fuentes, a coloured man in his escort, who killed Cayito, and others say it was Remigio himself, as had been planned. The truth is hard to get at, because Cayito was hit by three bullets, each one of which would have been fatal. The men who killed him had hidden themselves behind some bushes, and when they heard Cayito talking treason with the other colonels they shot his chest as full of holes as a colander.

That was the end of Cayito. And now the rumour-mongers and liars try to make out that he fought to the last and was as brave as a lion. Crap! He fell at once and never drew another breath. The Spanish heard that there had been some disturbance in the camp and didn't send out any columns that day. The following morning Felipe el Sol turned up to make sure that everything had gone as planned. Then he went back to General Duque, weeping crocodile tears, and told him about Cayito's death. Felipe had a talent for this sort of work.

Later the Spanish came out to the camp. Most of Cayito's men had already left, and the ones who stayed hid themselves to watch what happened. I saw it all myself, and then beat it as fast as I could. The Spanish arrived and planted their standard, then they dismounted and one of them took out a paper and read, 'An officer is dead because he wanted to honour the Spanish flag.' That's exactly what happened, and anyone who says different is lying. These things happen in wartime, which is the reason I say it kills men's trust in each other.

Thinking it over, it seems to me that Cayito did no more than follow the example of other officers who considered that surrendering at that time was not treachery because the revolt had failed with Maceo's death. Cayito may well have surrendered because of Maceo's death; he admired him. But all the same Cayito was a bad case, a traitor.

*

People still talk about Cayito and claim to see him all over the place. All I can say is they didn't know him, and if they had they wouldn't gab away so freely about him. I mean all that talk about lights moving at night in the forest and headless riders. Lots of people think this is Cayito's spirit risen to guard his buried treasure. Perhaps it is. I don't want to think about him. I'd rather it was someone else.

One day an old Negro came to me and told me he had seen lights that were the spirit of the bandit Cayito Alvarez. He was scared stiff. I looked at him and held my tongue. After all, nothing I said would have convinced him. But I thought to myself privately, Well, this idiot didn't know him when he was alive and he didn't fight under him either. If he had known Cayito he wouldn't be afraid of him dead. It was alive that he was dangerous.

After Cayito's death a large group of us from his regiment left for a place called Tranca, where we planned to shelter. We reached the place by nightfall. The following day we slept at Morota, a small place near La Esperanza. We still hadn't reached El Plátano, where the infantry and the riflemen, all brave Negroes, were camped. When we arrived there was a great uproar. All the men, some six hundred of them, wanted to know what had happened. We told them of the deaths of Cayito, Macagua and Núñez. They took it quite calmly. They seemed pleased but bewildered.

We organised ourselves as best we could, and the remaining officers gave the order for us to join forces with Brigadier Higinio Esquerra. I had already heard talk about him. People were always talking about the leaders, whether they knew about them or not, discussing the way they treated the soldiers and things like that. Then there was gossip about their women, and especially about whether so-and-so was a bandit or a decent man, so that when the order was given everyone thought to themselves, Off to fight for another bandit now! I didn't share this view, as a matter of fact; for all I knew, a bandit could have mended his ways.

I knew the sort of man Higinio was the minute I laid eyes on him: a man of few words, action suited him better. When we arrived he asked us various questions. I didn't take it on myself to answer, because I didn't think I had the right to. He struck me as brave and resolute. His whiskers were very striking because his skin was very white; he was a countryman like thousands of others, tall and thin. He took command of us at once, with such authority that everyone was a bit startled.

The first thing he did was court martial Cayito's brother-in-law, a man called Espinosa, whom we took prisoner because he was about to give himself up. Espinosa never imagined Higinio would treat him like that. I daresay he thought the whole thing was a fiesta. I remember his last request was that his silver watch, a beautiful thing, should be returned to his mother. Higinio himself took the watch and sent it to her. He was like that, a surprising character.

Then, that afternoon, he made a speech to the troops, to encourage them and raise their spirits. He told them the whole truth, how Cayito had been a traitor and many other men had been mixed up in the business. People looked each other up and down. A lot of them had already suspected something of the sort. Higinio read Cayito's private papers aloud, in public. I never saw such a silence, especially when he began to name the people involved. He named them all quite distinctly; Christian names, addresses and all. There were a lot of little colonels on that list, colonels who hadn't been brave enough to give themselves up.

The behaviour of our troop was an example to the rest; everyone who fought in that war knows this. That's how we were able to see the revolution through. I am sure almost all the troops would have behaved the same way in the same situation. We had guts, and we put the revolution before everything. That's the truth. However, there were plenty of colonels and other officers shitting off target every day. They did things children wouldn't do.

To gain a brigadier's respect you had to be a very honest, reliable man. This brigadier was a harsh man; he treated his soldiers brusquely and he would not tolerate any treachery. I respected him because there was something fine about him. He sent a group of us, a committee, to General Máximo Gómez. He insisted that this committee should only consist of the bravest, most loyal men, the ones who had dealt with Cayito's betrayal. It is true that the committee was composed of real fighters, men who would not gossip, but it was too small—they should have sent more men. You could count them on the fingers of one hand—Lieutenant Primitivo del Portal, Captain

Leonardo Fuentes, Commandant Zúñigas, Corporal Hugo Cuéllar, and Sub-lieutenant Remigio Pedroso. They went to see Máximo Gómez, who was at the La Campana camp at that time. He greeted them and talked to them, and then he promoted each of them one rank higher in recognition of their action. To my way of thinking, the whole troop should have got a medal, because they all helped in the revolt. Not that they could have decorated all of us, there were too many of us.

A few days later the officers returned with their new rank, and we had to welcome them. I am not certain even now that Máximo Gómez heard the full story of Cayito's death. I suspect they just told him as much as they thought he ought to know. Each of them wanted to make his mark, too. Besides, many people thought that Cayito had been killed for racialist reasons, officers in other battalions, I mean, because our own officers knew what sort of tangle there had been. At the time all our officers spoke as one man, they said, 'Yes, yes, yes.'

At the end of the war I heard lots of people saying, at the tops of their voices, 'The Negroes hated Cayito, they killed him.' All you can do when you hear this is keep silent or tell the truth. Since hardly anyone is likely to believe you, you keep silent. If you don't it only complicates things, or would have complicated them then, because nowadays no one keeps his mouth shut about anything.

Higinio never doubted Cayito's treachery, he knew the reasons for it. Every time he found a chance to say that our troop was an example to the rest, he said so. But in spite of this we never completely trusted him. Higinio respected those who respected him, and this was right. If a man doesn't respect you, you tell him to go to hell. We didn't trust him, though, ever since the day we learned that he had been a bandit. This shook our confidence in him, but we never threw the fact in his face. He always behaved like a patriot. The same thing applies to loose women and thieves and pimps; you imagine they must be the worst people around. But the worst people are the two-faced hypocrites.

We didn't see much fighting under Higinio. The only big engagement was at Arroyo Prieto, the rest was child's play. We fought several hours at Arroyo Prieto and won. It was a serious encounter though we only lost two or three men. Higinio fought well, and we resumed our march immediately afterwards.

Higinio liked a bit of fighting. A man who didn't fight was just a bit of useless decoration. Hell! That quiet sort of war with two or three little shots fired was worse than a pitched battle. Much worse!

*

I fell out with the officers a few times. When I was with Higinio at El Vizcaíno I got an order telling me to place myself at the disposal of Colonel Aranda as his orderly. I was furious. I went to Higinio at once and told him straight out, 'Look, I didn't join up to be orderly to anyone!' I was damned if I was going to help the colonel on with his leggings and clean his shoes! Higinio looked me in the face and said nothing. Then he turned his back, and I shot out of the place. The result was a fortnight's guard duties as punishment. You had to spend the whole time marching round the camp keeping an eye on things, you never got a wink of sleep. It was murder, what with the showers, the mud and slush, the mosquitoes. . . . If anyone didn't carry out the guard duties, they gave him the stocks. You might be going to fight and risk your skin, but they still punished you.

This Aranda was President of the War Veterans' Council after the war, and I saw him often. But he didn't remember me, at least he never spoke to me. My own opinion is he only fought in the war to escape justice, because the man was a criminal—he had killed his wife so as to get hold of her property. Aranda found himself another orderly, I was never given a job like that again, and Higinio and I never spoke to each other again. I lost my horse, reins, saddle—they were all given to Aranda's new orderly. They left me picked clean.

A few days later Corojito, the man who was made orderly instead, was swaggering about the camp showing off his horse. He was nothing but a toadying mulatto. This infuriated me, and that night I went off on foot to Jicotea. I had permission to go, to look for vegetables. I went with Juan Fabregas, who had been with me all through the war. Juan and I planned to break into the Spanish fort and seize two horses for ourselves. As we got near we saw that the entrance to the place was full of watchdogs. We took all our clothes off so the buggers couldn't smell us, and left them in a steelyard a little distance away. We just had to get hold of those horses so as not to end the war on foot!

We crept closer and closer, and as we reached the wire fence we saw the guard, but since we were dark-skinned and naked he evidently didn't see us. We went on and entered by the gate, creeping round the side of the sentry-box. The guard was asleep. We seized two horses and galloped out again. We didn't even need candles. Lots of people used to take candles when they went stealing, to frighten the dogs. I don't think dogs are any use at keeping watch. Geese are better. If you kept geese in a fort no one would dare try to break in. When the Spanish were here there were lots of houses where they kept geese for this purpose, but you never see them now.

When we got to the camp everyone stared at us in amazement and asked us, 'Negroes, where did you get those horses?' Juan answered, 'From the fort.' No one said anything, they probably didn't believe us. I went through the rest of the war with that horse, though. I never gave it a name, and I didn't look after it as well as the one I had before. It was a chestnut, a beautiful animal. After the war they gave me forty gold coins for it in the Caracas plantation.

I don't know what happened to Juan's horse. I did notice that the horse seemed to have given him a new lease of life. He was restless, he changed from one day to the next. One day I saw he was missing. Someone came to me and said, 'Listen, your friend has given himself up.' I paid no attention. I thought he must have gone off to hunt rats. But the days went by and I didn't catch a glimpse of him anywhere. At last I heard that he had surrendered to the Spanish. When I heard that I went cold all over. Then I fell into a rage, angry and contemptuous all at once. I went on fighting in the war for honour's sake, and I never saw Fabregas again. I looked for him at the end of the war, but I didn't find him.

*

A few weeks after Juan went, we marched to Santa Rosa, a big farm where there was a general barracks. That was where Martín Morúa Delgado joined us. Him I liked. He was swarthy and very tall, a red-haired, freckled mulatto. He never fought. He was made a lieutenant without having ever handled a machete. But he was a great man for reading, and he spent all his time in the barrack archives, arranging the bookshelves and sorting out the papers. He was that sort of man. For him it was a war of words. With the years he became famous, he even incited the Negro rebellion at Alto Songo. He was the cleverest man who went to Congress, and the greatest. Some whites used to say that he was a guerrilla, but they were Americans, scabs! They accused him of being a guerrilla just because of the colour of his skin.

The real guerrillas were stupid countrymen. Don't anyone try to tell me a man of letters would become a guerrilla. There were white guerrillas as well as black ones: Spanish ones, Canary Islanders, Cubans. I never saw a Chinese one.

The guerrilla tactics were different from those of the liberating army. Fire blazed from their eyes, they were men full of poison, rotten to the core. When they saw a group of *Mambises* they used to fall on them, and if they captured them they killed them all outright. When you fought face-to-face with Spaniards they never killed like that, in cold blood. They did things differently. I wouldn't say we fought on equal terms, though. They all had proper equipment, good mounts, reins, spurs, all the kit; we had almost nothing. Having all these things, the guerrillas thought they were superior.

I never met worse people in my life. Even now, all this time later, there are a few of them left on this island. Time has passed but they haven't changed, they still look at you with loathing. I know one who spends the whole time playing a guitar. He's a Negro, fat, big-bellied. Whenever I go by he bends his head and goes on playing. I don't look at him, to avoid trouble. But the day he tries anything silly I'll give him such a bashing he won't try the same game twice.

Before the war I knew lots of roughs, village roughs who lived by trickery of one sort or another. They were drifters, bums, and on Saturdays and Sundays they made trouble and boasted and got into fights and got drunk. Almost all those men, blacks as well as whites, became guerrillas. It was the only way out for them. They knew war wasn't a game, and they wanted safety. León was one of them, he acted as guide to the guerrillas and he was once the intimate, hand-in-glove friend of Valentín, the executioner, who must have bumped off a hell of a lot of people with the garrotte. That's what the guerrillas were like. So that anyone who tries to tell me Morúa was a guerrilla is a traitor and a liar.

When I think of those bastards, at a time when people like me were fighting against hunger, struggling through mud and all the foul stink of war, I feel like hanging the lot of them. But the sad thing is they never punished the guerrillas in Cuba. Máximo Gómez even tried to make them equal with the rest of us. He said this was only for convenience, but I'm telling you, that word 'convenience' doesn't impress me. I would have given them the same treatment the murderers in the last government got from the Revolution, put them up against a wall and shot the lot of them. And I never have and never will understand why Máximo Gómez said, in his speech at Quinta de los Molinos at the end of the war, that in Cuba there were neither victors nor vanquished. That was what he said. I heard him say it, because I was there at the time. It didn't go down well with anyone there. It meant that the guerrillas were put on the same level as the revolutionaries. People objected.

Colonel Isidro Acea, who was as black as a crow, got into his carriage and reached the demonstration after this remark of Gómez's. He arrived in a fury; that Negro wasn't afraid of anyone, he was a born fighter. He drove the carriage into Quinta de los Molinos, and when the people saw he was there they began shouting. Some people claim it was only the Negroes who shouted, but this isn't true. All patriots joined in the outcry. Isidro called for everyone to make way and got up on to the platform where Mario Menocal was standing. All the generals and the people respected him because he was brave and unceremonious. He went up to Menocal and said, 'Those people out there are going to come in.'

There were some iron grilles which prevented the crowd from entering, but here was Acea promising that they would be let in. Menocal looked at him in astonishment and said nothing. Máximo Gómez went on with his speech. Acea raised his voice and said to Menocal, 'Well, what's it to be, are they coming in or not? If they don't, I'll tear up those fences.' At that Menocal was forced to order the people to be admitted, and the stampede was appalling. Everyone rushed towards the platform. They carried Isidro Acea on their shoulders, because he had humiliated the leaders. Máximo Gómez finished his speech, but the people didn't pay much attention to him. He made a big mistake that day with his 'neither victors nor vanquished'.

The guerrillas ought to have been exterminated. Thinking back, Colonel Acea was a bit rash. I've never liked show-offs, so at the time I swallowed Gómez's words and didn't protest. I thought Acea's action was an abuse, but in war you never know who is going to take the initiative next. Everyone listening to the speech was astonished by the Colonel's arrival. I remember all this clearly, because I had just arrived in Havana with the rest of the troops. It must have been about a week after I reached the capital, and it was the first time I had ever been there. It seemed strange to me at first, though I got used to it gradually, but I never really liked it. I liked the countryside and the forest best.

*

Havana in those days of victory was like a fairground, and the Negroes enjoyed themselves to the hilt. I was surprised to find such a large Negro population in Havana; everywhere you looked you saw a Negro. The women were so pleased and happy that the war was over that they started coming out into the street. Well, what can you expect? I must have had more than fifty Negresses in one week. Almost all the guerrillas' wives slept with the liberators. One of them came to me and said, 'Take me with you, my husband was a guerrilla,' but I left her because she was getting on a bit. Every time a chick went past I'd cast my line and grab her. I didn't need to chat them up, they just offered themselves ripe for the picking. They took one look at your liberator's uniform and your machete, and this seemed to excite them.

Not being much of a one for fiestas, I usually wanted to take them off straight away for another sort of fun and games, and many of them were ready and willing. The others used to drag me along to the waterside district, where there was a fountain and a street with lamps and cargo boats close enough to see quite clearly. There was more dancing there than anywhere else in town, rumbas, which they played on little boxes and on drums which they held between their knees. The streets and the court-yards of the houses were full of stools for people to sit on while old and young danced till they dropped. The clubs of the *náñigos* were all lit up.

There were fights and shootings and stabbings and quarrels of all sorts. People kept inventing new rumbas to sing. Anyone who wasn't satisfied with the way Cuba was governed used to sing this one about Santa Eulalia, which sounds like a prayer:

Santa Eulalia is looking
to see how the Cubans rule
and it makes her feel sad.
Ay, Dios, the Queen is weeping!

I felt happy. I'd never believed the war could end. It was like when I'd been in the forest and heard that slavery had been abolished. It's hard to believe these things. During the war I'd got used to going about naked, seeing bayonets almost every day and fleeing from the guerrillas. When they told me an armistice had been declared, I took no notice. But Havana convinced me completely. The whole town seemed to have gone crazy with joy. The people cheered Máximo Gómez in the streets and kissed his jacket. There wasn't a Cuban who didn't go round shouting, 'Long Live Free Cuba!'

People shook hands with complete strangers in the streets and threw off their hats and scarves. I can't describe all this properly because I was too involved, and so I don't remember it all that clearly. But I remember about the clothes and hats and the styles which the Americans introduced. They said that men ought to go about with their heads bare, and some people followed their example. I never liked this fashion—the only time I took my hat off was to go to sleep. One's head should always be decently covered, it seems to me rude to go about exhibiting one's cranium all over the place. The

Americans didn't give a damn, they did just as they pleased, especially the tourists, who were a bunch of thieves.

*

The capital was a strange place, you saw the most vulgar, garish things. It was the best place in the world if you liked novelty. There was so much entertainment that everyone got quite lightheaded, what with the drunkenness and everything else. I played about a bit with the women, but in spite of everything I kept my head, I stayed the same. After a few days you didn't know who to trust. I stayed in a wooden house belonging to some people I knew. A lot of the liberators slept in strangers' houses at that time, the whole city opened its doors. Havana was a hospitable place then. But I wasn't taken in by stories of coloured lights and drinking and cheap women. I didn't like all that, and this is one of the things everyone knows about me; I didn't approve of the way the people in the capital carried on. And the pimps were a bad lot, men living on air and graft—in Havana that is, because you don't find pimps anywhere else.

Laws are stricter in the countryside, the laws of men who see things as they are. But in the city the pimps were up to every kind of trick, strolling about, mocking, making trouble. They wore shirts with two letters embroidered on them—HR—of fine long-lasting cotton. Their shoes were good, too, but ugly; of deerhide or carpeting. People called them slippers, and they were a Spanish style.

The good-for-nothings used to tie a red scarf round their necks to impress women. They knocked the whores about and beat them up all over the place. That was the first thing I saw when I got off the train at Havana: smart-looking fellows with shirts belted in at the waist and French knives, beating up streetwalkers. They obviously couldn't see what a spectacle they made, or they'd have dropped this habit of slopping about in slippers and hitting whores. The only people who tried to check this sort of thing were the Americans, who sent them to some place outside Havana or set them breaking stones in the street. They had to break the stones under a hot sun and get bruised backs, the sons-of-bitches!

That's why I didn't like the city life. Of course, I was used to the country. We found everything in the city strange and new, but I suppose the city people would have thought the country was hell. What upset them all most was the American checkmate. The people of Havana seem to have thought the Americans were coming there for fun, but then they realised their mistake, that all they wanted was the biggest slice of the cake. The mass of people just sat back and let it happen. There were even some people who rejoiced that the Americans had taken the initiative. They used to say, and some still do, that the best thing about the war was the American intervention.

I remember an incident about that time to do with a priest who suffered the worst humiliation I have ever seen. The Americans said he was a rogue and set him to work breaking stones in the streets, in his soutane and everything, right in the centre of Havana, near where the presidential palace stands today.

All the old people know about this, and they know that the Americans were responsible. I went to see the man because I just didn't believe such a thing could happen. I got up early and rushed to the square where they told me the priest was working. I saw him straight away, working in the hot sun with his soutane sticking to his body. Knowing how soft most of the priests were, I could hardly believe my eyes. But this is perfectly true, it isn't a tall story. When women went by and caught sight of him, they used to cross themselves because they couldn't believe what they saw. I had to pinch myself to make sure I wasn't dreaming. Nothing more was heard about the priest after that. Personally, I think he must still haunt the place, hoping to avenge himself.

The Americans didn't like the Negroes much. They used to shout, 'Nigger, nigger,' and burst out laughing. If you joined in the joke they went on trying to annoy you, but if you took no notice they left you alone. They never tried to interfere with me; I couldn't stomach them, and that's a fact. I never joked with them, I gave them the slip whenever I could. After the war ended the arguments began about whether the Negroes had fought or not. I know that ninety-five per cent of the blacks fought in the war, but they started saying it was only seventy-five per cent. Well, no one got up and told them they were lying, and the result was the Negroes found themselves out in the streets—men brave as lions, out in the streets. It was unjust, but that's what happened.

[216]

There wasn't even one per cent of Negroes in the police force, because the Americans came out with this theory that if you give the Negro power and educate him, he'll turn round and harm the whites. So they segregated the Negroes completely. The rest of the Cubans kept quiet and did nothing, and there things remained until today, when they must have changed, because I have seen white men with black women and black men with white women—which is more astonishing—in the streets and cafés, all over the place.

Although Morúa and Campos Marquetti tried to solve the problem by giving various government jobs to Negroes, jobs as watchmen, porters, postmen, when the army disbanded the Negro revolutionaries found they couldn't stay in the city and went back to the countryside, to work in the cane-fields and tobacco plantations, anything rather than work in offices. Even the guerrillas, traitors though they were, had better chances than we did. It's true, all this, not worth arguing about. General Maceo himself would have had to hang a whole lot of people in the forest before he could have achieved anything.

Later everyone said that the Americans were the real villains. I agree, they were the biggest ones, but remember that the white Creoles were just as guilty, because they let themselves be buggered about on their own soil, all of them, from colonels down to cleaners. Why didn't the Cuban people rebel during the *Maine* affair? Any fool here knew that the Americans blew up the *Maine* themselves so as to get into the war. If the people here had risen, everything would have been different and a lot of things would never have happened. But at the crucial moment no one said or did anything. Máximo Gómez, who must have known what was going on, held his peace and took the secret to his grave. This is what I think, and may I drop dead if I'm lying.

*

I used to know more things once, facts which history has covered up. I used to talk everything over with my friends when we were alone. But my head's too much of a muddle these days. Even so, I remember the most important things, although it can only be a handful of times that I have ever discussed them with anyone. I remember once, when I said that the story of the American intervention in Santiago was a lie and that they hadn't taken the place on their own, someone started fighting with me so as not to get into trouble with the authorities. It's good that you can talk about everything now. Anyway, the truth is that Calixto García won the day at Santiago. The Spanish officer in command of the place was called Vara el Rey. The Americans bombarded the place, but it was Calixto García who attacked Vara el Rey's men by land and destroyed them. Then the Americans ran up their flag to show that they had taken the city. What a farce! Vara el Rey with five hundred men, slaughtered a whole mass of Americans. The worst thing was that the American commanding officer ordered that no Cuban should enter the city. That was what made everyone's blood boil. When the Cubans found they weren't allowed in, they began to resent the

Americans and Calixto García said some hard things to them. Frankly, I prefer the Spaniards to the Americans, the Spaniards in Spain, that is. Everyone should stay in their own country, though the fact is I don't like the Americans even in their own country.

In the war the Spaniards used to say to the women, 'Here, Pancha, your father is shooting at me, but here's some food for you, damn you!' They weren't all that bloodthirsty. But the Americans were the bloody limit. They used to dig a hole and throw the food down it. Everyone knew about this, they saw it. Wood, Theodore Roosevelt, and the other one whose name I've forgotten, the whole pack of degenerates who ruined this country!

*

In Cienfuegos, round about the year 1899, some *Mambises* drew their machetes on some American soldiers because the bastards were trying to lay all the Creole girls as if they were so much meat in the market. They wouldn't have respected their own mothers. They would pass a house and catch sight of a pretty woman at the window or in the doorway, and they'd go up and say, 'Foky, foky, Margarita,' and the next thing you knew, they would be in. I saw this happen in Cienfuegos. With this 'foky, foky' talk, they got themselves a packet of trouble. We found out what was going on and went along to watch. The Americans wore yellow uniforms, well pressed, and they were nearly always drunk. Claudio Sarría, who had been a sergeant, gave the order to use the machetes, and we rushed along there in a fury.

We kept watch for a while, and sure enough, a group of Americans started making trouble in a street near the wharf. They got talking to the women, and pinched their bottoms and laughed. I don't think I felt as angry at any time in the war as I did then. We went up to them with our machetes drawn and forced them to get out. Some of them ran down to the wharf to where their boat was, and the rest rushed up to the Escambray hills like bats out of hell. They never bothered a woman there again.

When they went out they used to have an officer with them; they went into the cafés escorted like schoolboys. But that day all of us who took part in that incident were risking our skins. Mind you, they have done many worse things since, and nobody has protested.

The Americans wheedled their way into possession of Cuba, but they don't really deserve all the blame. It was the Cubans who obeyed them who were the really guilty people. There is still a lot to be unravelled there, I am sure. But it would take till Kingdom come to uncover the whole mess. But it should be done, because today they've got a finger in the pie all over the world.

After the war the Cuban colonels gave MacKinley an open invitation to do what he liked with this island. There was some land belonging to the Marquis de Santa Lucía where Santa Marta is now. From what I gather he left this land to be shared out among the revolutionaries. What happened was that the Americans divided the land with Menocal—the dirtiest swindle of the whole war! Menocal kept his mouth shut and took his ease. He was more American than MacKinley himself, and everyone disliked him because of it. He was a business patriot, not a real one.

And there are thousands of other things like this which it would take too long to tell. I used to think about everything more when I was younger, but then I had to take a hold on myself because it was making me feverish. I have bouts of thinking still, but I don't think things out for fun, they just stick to me and it would take an earthquake to shake them off.

What has saved me is that I keep my mouth shut. You can't trust people. If you trust people too much you're finished. After the war, when the troops came to Havana, I watched them closely. A lot of them wanted to stay on and be soft and comfortable in the city. Well, the ones who did came off worse than if they had gone back to the forest. I say worse because then the pushing and shoving and deceptions and lies began. 'Negro, you are going to make your fortune here!' but, shit, he would be the first to die of hunger! That's why when the leaders said, 'The war is over, now we must all set to work,' I took my bundle and went to the railway station near the wall of Havana—I still remember it now—and got on a train for Las Villas. That's where I asked to go to at the ticket office. Las Villas is the best part of Cuba. Anyway, I was born there.

The guerrillas remained in the offices because they could do figures, stupid things like that, or had a pretty daughter, or cash to spare. I went back to the country without a cent in my pocket. I gave myself a temporary discharge.

[221]

When I reached Remedios I met some acquaintances of mine, then I went on to Cruces and began working on the San Agustín Maguaraya plantation, the same work as before. It seemed as though everything had gone back in time. I began on the conveyor belt, but later I moved to the mixer because the work was easier there and you earned thirty-six pesos a month. I lived alone in a palm-house until I felt the urge to get myself a woman. I had one for a time, but not long because things got too difficult. Then I got rid of her and went back to living alone.

I didn't make friends at Maguaraya. I've never liked thugs or roughs. No one talked to me much there. And I must admit I didn't let my hair down. Every cripple has his own way of walking.

I worked all day, and at night I went home to rest and get rid of the ticks, which are the worst damned creatures on earth. I visited almost all the villages of Las Villas. I became a pedlar, a night-watchman, the lot! I learned every job so no one could get the better of me.

*

I got to Havana one day and found that Máximo Gómez was dead. When a man dies the people soon forget him. The only thing I heard anyone say about Gómez was that his spirit often appeared down by the Quinta de los Molinos, and that the place was full of ghosts.

I walked through a park and saw that they had set him up there on a bronze horse; I kept on down the hill, and about half a mile further on I found they had stuck Maceo up on another bronze horse. The difference was that Gómez faced north towards the United States and Maceo looked towards the town and the people.

Everyone should think about this. It tells the whole story, and I spend all my time saying so because truth cannot be silenced. Even if I had to die tomorrow I would not give up my pride. If I could, I would come right out and tell the whole story now. Before, when I was naked and dirty in the forest, I saw the Spanish soldiers looking as neat as Chinese characters, with the finest weapons, and I had to keep quiet. That's why I say I don't want to die, so I can fight in all the battles to come. And I'm not going into the trenches or using any of those modern weapons. A machete will do for me.